D0418910

CREATIVE
Christening Cakes

Anne Smith

MEREHURST

ACKNOWLEDGEMENTS

I would like to thank my husband Clive, my greatest critic and adviser, for his perseverence in transferring all my illegible scrawl into readable script on his word processor, also my two patient children, Helen and David, who have both been generous with their encouragement and understanding.

My thanks also to Pauline of "Mrs Pickwick", who has been both a friend and local supplier of all my sugarpaste materials for many years, also Jennie and Norma of "A Piece of Cake" whose friendly and quick 24-hour service has been invaluable in helping me complete the book on schedule.

Finally, I would like to thank the local shopkeepers in my village of Timsbury, in particular Colin Robinson of the "8 to 8" shop, who has been so helpful in supplying me with the appropriate-sized boxes for the transportation of my cakes to London.

Published in 1995 by Merehurst Limited
Ferry House, 51-57 Lacy Road, Putney, London SW15 1PR
Copyright © 1995 Merehurst Limited
ISBN 1 85391 472 X

A catalogue record for this book is available from the British Library.

Edited by Donna Wood
Designed by Maggie Aldred
Photography by Clive Streeter
Illustrations by Anne Smith and King & King Design Associates
Typesetting by Peter A. Lovell
Colour separation by Global Colour, Malaysia
Printed in Italy by Canale & C.S.p.A.

Contents

Introduction

I have thoroughly enjoyed producing a book that celebrates such a joyous occasion as the baptism of a baby. In doing so it has been my intention to create a book that will appeal to parents of varying tastes – from the fun-loving to the strictly formal.

A step-by-step method has been used to enable beginners to cope with confidence but I have also tried to offer some advanced work that will appeal to the more experienced cake decorator. Many different techniques such as crimper work, cut work, simple pastillage, bas relief, painting on sugarpaste and cocoa painting, have been incorporated.

Whatever their level of ability, I hope that every reader from novice to experienced cake decorator will find something here to interest and inspire them.

Basic Recipes

SUGARPASTE

This paste is used for general-purpose decoration throughout this book.

15g (½ oz) gelatine
60ml (2 fl oz/¼ cup) cold water
125ml (4 fl oz) liquid glucose
22g (¾ oz) glycerine
1kg (2 lb) icing (confectioner's) sugar

Soak the gelatine in the cold water and place over hot water until dissolved and clear. Do not allow the gelatine to boil. Add the glucose and glycerine to the gelatine and stir until melted. Add the mixture to the sieved icing (confectioner's) sugar. Knead to a soft consistency.

MODELLING PASTE

This paste is malleable and easily stretched which makes it ideal for bas relief work.

280g (9 oz/2¼ cups) icing (confectioner's) sugar
1 tbsp gum tragacanth
1 tsp liquid glucose
6 tsp cold water
about 315g (10 oz) sugarpaste

Sieve the sugar with the gum tragacanth. Add the liquid glucose and cold water and mix well. Knead to form a soft dough, then combine with an equal weight of sugarpaste. Leave for 24 hours before using. If the paste is too dry, knead in a little white fat (shortening) or egg white. If the paste is sticky, add a little cornflour (cornstarch).

FLOWER PASTE

There are many variations on the following recipe for flower paste but this is a reliable one to start with.

440g (14 oz/3½ cups) icing (confectioner's) sugar
60g (2 oz/½ cup) cornflour (cornstarch)
3 tsp gum tragacanth
5 tsp cold water
2 tsp powdered gelatine
3 tsp white fat (shortening)
2 tsp liquid glucose
white of 1 egg, string removed

Sift together the icing (confectioner's) sugar and cornflour (cornstarch) in the bowl of a heavy duty mixer. Sprinkle over the gum tragacanth. Place the mixer over a large pan of boiling water. Cover the top with a dry cloth and then with a plate. Put the cold water in a small glass bowl and sprinkle over the gelatine. Leave to sponge.

Half-fill a small saucepan with water and heat to just below boiling point. Place the bowl of sponged gelatine, the container of liquid glucose and the beater from the mixer in the water. Heat gently until the gelatine is clear. Remove the bowl of gelatine from the pan and stir in the liquid glucose and the white fat (shortening). Continue to stir until the fat is melted. When the icing (confectioner's) sugar feels warm, take the bowl off the pan of boiling water, dry the bottom and place in the mixer. Remove the beater from the other pan, dry and assemble the mixer. Add the gelatine solution and the egg white to the sugar, cover the bowl with a cloth and turn the mixer to the slowest speed. Mix until all the ingredients are combined and the paste is a dull beige colour.

Turn the mixer to maximum and beat for about 5-10 minutes, or until the paste becomes white and stringy. Remove the paste from the bowl and place in a clear polythene bag. Place the bag in an airtight container and refrigerate for at least 24 hours before using.

To use the flower paste, cut off a small piece at a time and work with your fingers until it has an elastic consistency. If the paste is dry, add more egg white or white fat (shortening); if the paste is too sticky, try adding a little more cornflour (cornstarch).

GELATINE PASTE

This paste can be cut to shape and size and used to make a gelatine plaque which can then be decorated.

1 tbsp gelatine
60ml (2 fl oz) cold water
1 tsp white fat (shortening)
1 tsp liquid glucose
500g (1 lb/4½ cups) icing (confectioner's) sugar

Soak the gelatine in the cold water and place over a pan of hot water until dissolved and clear. Do not allow the gelatine to boil. Add the fat (shortening) and glucose to the gelatine and stir until melted. Add this mixture to the sieved sugar and knead together to form a firm paste. Add a little more water if the paste is too stiff.

To help the keeping quality of the paste, pat the surface all over with a little water then place in a polythene bag. Store in a cool place; it is not necessary to refrigerate this paste. Leave for two hours before using.

GUM ARABIC

4 tbsp rosewater
1 tbsp gelatine crystals
(mix any quantity in 4 : 1 ratio)

Place the rosewater in a cup over hot water. Sprinkle the gelatine into the cup, do not allow the mixture to overheat. Stir until all the crystals have dissolved. Strain the mixture through a fine sieve lined with muslin. Allow the mixture to drip through gradually. Place in a small glass jar.

ROYAL ICING

500g (1 lb) icing (confectioner's) sugar
3 tsp powdered albumen (egg white substitute)
75ml (2½ fl oz) water

Sieve the icing sugar. Add the powdered albumen to the water. Initially the albumen will form lumps but with gentle stirring the lumps will disappear. Strain the liquid through a fine strainer into the icing sugar. Mix well (if using a mixer, 10 minutes on slow speed) until the icing forms firm peaks. Always cover the icing with a damp cloth to prevent the surface drying out and forming a crust. Any excess icing can be frozen. Re-beat when thawed, until the mixture forms firm peaks again.

Decorating Techniques

PREPARING AND COVERING THE CAKE

PREPARING THE CAKE SURFACE

Take care not to damage the corners of the cake when removing it from the tin. Turn the cake upside-down so that the bottom of the cake provides a flat top surface. Stick the cake to the board with a little marzipan (almond paste) softened with warm apricot glaze. If the edges of the cake do not sit level on the cakeboard, make a sausage of marzipan and push into the gaps with a palette knife. Fill any visible holes and repair any damaged corners with marzipan. Smooth over with a palette knife until all the damaged areas are level.

Gently heat some apricot glaze, sieve and brush over the surface of the cake to ensure that the marzipan will adhere to the surface.

APPLYING MARZIPAN (almond paste)

Knead the marzipan on a clean, dry work surface until pliable using a circular motion. The edge of the paste is brought into the middle, forming pleats, while the lower surface remains quite smooth. When rolling the marzipan out, this smooth side should be uppermost.

Roll out on a surface evenly dusted with icing (confectioner's) sugar. Never use flour or cornflour (cornstarch) as these can cause fermentation to occur.

When rolling out, keep the marzipan moving so that it does not stick to the work surface. Do not turn the marzipan over as for pastry, but keep this smooth surface uppermost until the desired shape and size has been achieved. Roll out the marzipan to the same shape as the cake, this makes it easier to handle when placing on the cake and avoids wastage. The use of spacers at this stage ensures that the overall thickness of the marzipan is

▲ *Any holes in the cake surface or damaged edges can be repaired with marzipan.*

consistent. Measure the cake with a piece of string, take it up on one side, across the top and down the other side. The marzipan should be rolled out just a little larger than this measurement.

To apply, lift up the left side of the marzipan and lay it over your right arm. Lift up your arm and drape the marzipan against the side of the cake; the right side of the marzipan should be on the board. Drape over the top of the cake, transfer the marzipan to the left hand and support it while you remove any air bubbles by brushing your right hand across the top of the cake.

Skirt out the corners and, using the flat of your hand, smooth the marzipan to the sides of the cake using an upward movement. If a downward movement is used, it drags the marzipan and weakens the paste causing cracks to appear on the top edges and corners. Use smoothers to eliminate any finger marks and bumps. Smooth any cracks from the corners and upper edges using the warmth of your hand. Place the flat edge of a cranked palette knife against the cake at the base and cut away the excess marzipan.

▲ *Lift the marzipan and drape it over the top of the cake, then skirt out the corners.*

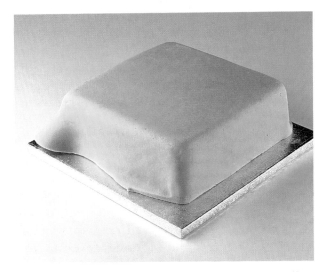

▲ *Smooth out any cracks from the corners. Cut off the excess marzipan from the base of the cake.*

APPLYING SUGARPASTE

A cake does not really need to be covered with marzipan first. If anyone dislikes the taste of marzipan, then the cake may be covered with two layers of sugarpaste instead. The first layer is usually thinner and for the best results should be allowed to skin and harden before applying the second layer. Both layers are applied in the same way.

Knead the sugarpaste as for marzipan and add any colour at this stage.

Roll out the sugarpaste on a light dusting of icing (confectioner's) sugar. Avoid using too much sugar as this will dry the paste and make it crack. Use spacers to keep the thickness of the paste uniform. Measure the cake as for marzipan and roll out the sugarpaste a little larger than the measurement.

Before applying the paste, sterilize the surface of the cake by moistening all over with clear alcohol such as gin, vodka or kirsch. Using the palm of the hand or a brush, make sure the entire surface is moist. If there are any dry areas the paste will not stick to the marzipan and could cause air bubbles.

Lift and drape the paste over the cake using the same technique as for marzipan. Skirt out the corners and smooth out any creases using an upward movement. Use smoothers to rub over the top and sides of the cake and to round the corners.

If any air bubbles have been trapped under the paste, insert a clean needle into the bubble at an angle. Smooth over with your hand to expel the air and rub with a smoother. If the pin hole is still visible, this can be easily hidden with a small dot of royal icing of the same colour piped into the hole and then wiped away to leave a smooth finish.

Use a cranked palette knife to trim away the excess paste. Smooth over the cut area. Wipe away any sugar on the board and store the cake in a dry place until the sugarpaste has skinned.

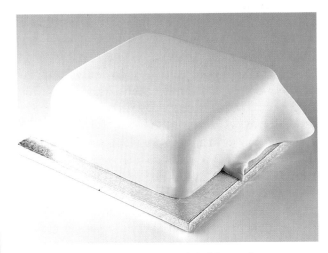

▲ *Use a cranked palette knife held upright to trim away the excess sugarpaste.*

Making and applying a
GARRETT FRILL

Special round or straight cutters with scalloped edges are used to create the Garrett frill.

To begin, knead 1 tsp gum tragacanth into 250g (8 oz) sugarpaste and leave for at least 24 hours. This special mix will enable the frill to keep its lift without drooping when placed on the cake. As the paste is rolled so thinly for each frill, only small amounts – about 60g (2 oz) – are normally needed. The rest can be refrigerated until required.

Frills are easier to place on a firm surface, so allow the sugarpaste on the cake to dry for a few days.

If a crimped edge is desired, the frill must be applied when the paste on the cake is soft. This crimping can disguise a poor edge.

Before applying the frill, pipe a snail trail around the base of the cake. It is important that this edge is finished off neatly as it will be visible at the points where the frill lifts.

Roll the paste very thinly and cut out a circle with a scalloped cutter. Remove a centre circle of paste. The size of this removed circle determines the width of the frill. Cut out a large inside circle for narrow frill and small inside circle for a deeper one.

Cut the frill and open up the circle until fairly straight. Be careful with the middle area of the upper edge as this is the weakest point.

Scribe a line onto the cake where the frill is to be attached. Place the frill near the edge of the board. Put a cocktail stick (toothpick) halfway up the paste and, putting an index finger on top of the stick, rotate it. As the stick moves over the paste it

◀ *Cut out a circle of very thin paste with the cutter, remove the centre and open out the frill.*

▼ *The edges of the frill can be flounced by rolling a cocktail stick over the paste.*

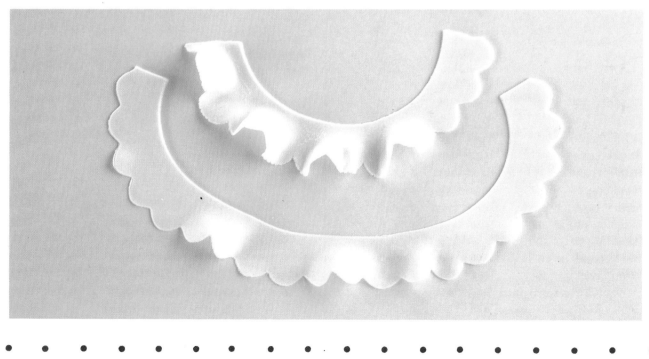

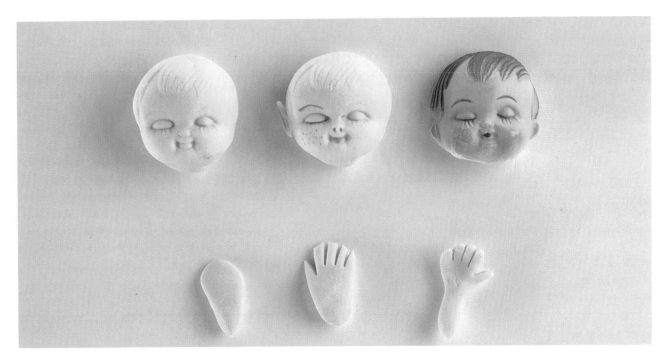

▲ *Building up the features of a baby's head made from a doll's head mould, and making a hand.*

will make the frill. Repeat along the entire edge of the paste. For a more definite lift use a flouncing or anger tool rotated gently in the same manner on the edge of the paste.

Moisten the cake below the scribed line with a little water and attach the frill. Smooth over the upper edge gently with your thumb. Raise the frill with the end of a paintbrush to give lift where needed. When adding the second frill, butt the edges together and turn under the extreme edge of the frill so that it appears to form a natural fold.

Several methods can be used to finish off the upper edge of the frill. Try piping a snail trail, cross-stitch or dots. Small lace sections can look very attractive. Plunger cutter flowers also produce a pleasing effect.

The cake's colour scheme can be emphasized by graduating the shade of each layer of frills, starting with the darkest shade for the lowest layer, as in *Frilled Cradle*, page 37. Petal dusting powder can also be applied to the edge of the frill.

BABY'S HEADS AND HANDS

Many of the cakes in this book feature babies in cradles, in beds, or in baskets, with their heads and hands visible to varying degrees.

A foolproof way of making the head is to find a small doll (or Christmas angel) and push the face into a piece of modelling or gelatine paste to make a mould. Once hardened, a ball of flesh-coloured modelling paste can be pushed into the mould, then the features emphasized and improved with an anger tool. The head can then be painted and dusted as shown above.

To make a hand, start with a spade-shaped piece of flesh-coloured paste, then cut a small V with scissors for the thumb. Make three further cuts for the fingers, pull the fingers as for pulled flowers and round them off. Taper the wrist and stroke from fingers towards the palm with a ball tool to curl.

LETTERING

Baby's names and messages can be added to the cakes in a number of ways; by tracing the letters from an alphabet of your choice, making a template, then piping on the name, or by making your own italic lettering by fixing two pencils together with an elastic band, keeping the point of one slightly higher than the other so that both make a mark when writing. This method was used to make a template for *Julia's Rattle*, page 16. Alternatively, shop-bought alphabet cutters can be used to stamp out the letters from sugarpaste (see *Frilled Cradle*, page 37 and *Benjamin*, page 67).

Mouse in a Cradle

A sprig of summery apple blossom suspends this baby mouse.

CAKE AND DECORATION

20cm (8 in) round fruit cake · apricot glaze
1kg (2 lb) marzipan (almond paste) · 1kg (2 lb)
sugarpaste · chestnut, paprika, cream and
blueberry food colourings · gum arabic · small
amount of royal icing · blue dusting powder (petal
dust/blossom tint) · 60g (2 oz) modelling paste
(bas relief paste) · small spray of seasonal flowers
scrap of narrow ribbon for hanging basket
1m (1 yd) ribbon for board edge

EQUIPMENT

28cm (11 in) round cakeboard · round plaque
cutter · gelatine plaque (see page 5) · scriber
small blossom plunger cutter · anger tool · ball
tool · cotton · carnation cutter · piping tubes
(tips) · fine paintbrush · template (see page 12)

TIP
*Make seasonal
flowers to suit
the time of year
of the birth or
baptism. Try
catkins or lilac for
spring, fir cones
for autumn or
holly with berries
for a winter baby.*

1 Cover the cake with marzipan, then sugarpaste. Using a round deep cutter, remove a section from the top of the cake while the sugarpaste is still soft. Smooth away any marks made while removing the shape.

2 Make some gelatine paste, see page 5, and cut out a plaque using the same cutter. Allow to dry.

3 To make the bas relief mouse for the inset, mark the image onto the plaque using a scriber or a fine pencil. Colour bas relief modelling

paste with chestnut, paprika and cream to create the wicker basket. Roll out finely and cut out the inside of the hood. Create a woven effect by indenting curved marks using one petal of a small blossom cutter. Mark, so that the indentations fan out and are not simply arranged in straight lines.

4 Roll out a thick sausage shape. Flatten with a rolling pin and cut out an arc shape. Round the outer edges using the fingers so that they curve and touch the base of the plaque. Push the inner edge of the hood against

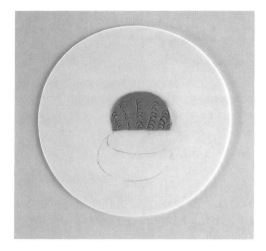

▲ *Create a woven effect on the hood using one petal of a plunger cutter.*

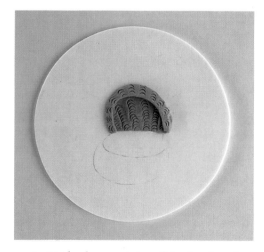

▲ *Apply the outer rim of the hood and mark as before to resemble basket weave.*

the thumb using an anger tool. Mark again with the blossom cutter as shown. Roll out two thin strips of paste, twist them together quite tightly and glue to the edge of the hood to complete.

5 To make the pillow, take a small ball of white paste and flatten with your thumb. Square off the sides and tweak out the corners. Using a ball tool, indent and flatten for the mouse's head. Remove excess paste. Attach to the inside hood of basket.

6 To make the mouse, colour some sugarpaste light brown, make a ball, then a cone. Indent an eye shape using the end of an anger tool. Make a hole in which to place the upper ear. The ear on the underside of the head is made by making a small ball, then a cone. Flatten it by pressing between the thumb and forefinger.

7 Make the upper ear by using two slightly larger balls of paste, one brown, one a fleshy pink. Flatten both balls as before. Place the pink flattened ball slightly below the brown one so that the pink is edged with brown. Squeeze the bottom edge together and cut away the excess. Glue the base and place in the ear.

▼ *The components need to complete the central image.*

Actual size

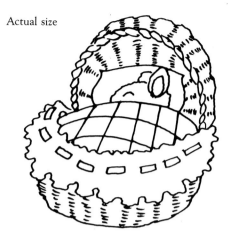

8 Simulate fur using a scalpel. Make whiskers from cotton stiffened with sugar syrup (a high proportion of sugar dissolved in water).

9 To make the bedspread and lower basket, roll out paste so that the lower edge is quite thick. The paste should diminish as you roll away from you. Mark quilt lines on the bedspread when it has been pushed into shape. Place over the base of the basket and butt it up to the bottom edge of the plaque. Curve around the bedspread. Mark basket lines as before.

10 For the lace frill use a carnation cutter. Cut out the lace pattern using piping tubes. Frill the bottom curved edge – this will make the straight piece of paste curve.

11 Insert fine ribbon while the basket and frill paste are still soft. Complete by painting on finishing touches to give tone and depth. Dust the coverlet with a darker blue dusting powder in the corners and add lines to give a 3D effect. Attach more ribbon to each side of the basket with royal icing and join together above the basket.

12 Make a sprig of flowers, or use a fabric sprig. Wire it to form a branch but leave a slight gap where the branch will meet the ribbon. Attach the branch to the plaque with royal icing. Make a small bow and attach to the gap on the branch.

Cradle Garland

This is a very easy cake to make as there is no wiring involved when making the flowers. It is simple in design and suitable for most beginners.

CAKE AND DECORATION

23cm (9 in) oval fruit cake · apricot glaze
1.25kg (2½ lb) marzipan (almond paste)
1.25kg (2½ lb) sugarpaste · 30g (1 oz) modelling paste (bas relief paste) · 30g (1 oz) flower paste
assorted dusting powders (petal dust/blossom tint) · assorted paste colours for flowers
30g (1 oz) royal icing, coloured Christmas green
gum arabic · piping gel · 2m (2 yd) narrow ribbon
1m (1 yd) ribbon for board edge

EQUIPMENT

28cm (11 in) oval cakeboard · scriber · ball tool
cocktail stick (toothpick) · no. 2 piping tube (tip)
no. 1 paintbrush · miniature plunger cutter
rose petal cutters · small daisy cutter · silk
stamens · tweezers · pieces of foam sponge
templates (see page 74-75)

1 Cover the cake with marzipan, then white sugarpaste. When the sugarpaste is dry, scribe the image of the garland onto the cake. Do not bother to mark on the ribbon bows or rose petals. Paint the small leaves on the cake surface using gooseberry and Christmas green colours.

2 Using the cutwork method (see page 40), colour a grape-sized piece of modelling paste pale blue. Using the inner cradle shape template, roll out the paste thinly and cut out using the template. Apply to the cake surface.

3 Cut out the pillow shape from white paste, the baby's head from flesh-coloured paste and bed cover from white paste. To colour the paste for the cradle, add champagne, brown, and peach petal dusts to the modelling paste. Roll this paste out a little more thickly so that it sits higher than the previous shapes.

4 To make the drapes at the top and side of the cradle, roll out the paste as thinly as possible. Cut out and ball the edges so that they are really fine. For the top frill, roll the edge with a cocktail stick. Fold the edges under and place in position.

5 For the side drapes, again ball the cut edges. Turn the outer edges under and make folds as shown. Arrange around the cradle until a natural effect is achieved. Glue in place. Attach the bottom of the drapes below the bow using the same method. Roll out some white modelling paste quite thinly. Cut a scalloped edge with a cocktail stick and attach to the bottom

▲ *First attach the ribbon tails, then the loops. Lastly add a ball for the centre.*

of the coverlet and the top of the cradle edge.

6 For the bows, cut out the two tails (see template) and soften the edges with a ball tool. Butt against the drape and twist and curl attractively. Make the loops using the template. Soften the edges. Glue together and attach between the tails. Make a small ball for the centre of the bow and flatten into place. Make a further bow for the top of the cradle. Paint small blue spots on the coverlet. Paint on the baby's hair and add a few strands on the pillow to create a softer look. Paint on the features.

7 For the larger rose leaves, add ¼ tsp piping gel to the royal icing. Fill the piping bag and outline the leaf. Draw the icing towards the middle of the leaf with a no. 1 paintbrush. Clean the brush and draw it down the centre to form the vein.

8 For the roses, use rose petal cutters of various sizes. Colour a grape-sized piece of flower paste with a touch of claret. Roll out the paste very thinly, ball the edges to give movement to each petal and attach in place.

9 For the rosebuds, cut out two petals, then ball and soften the edges. Place both petals, slightly overlapping, one on top of the other.

Colour a grape-sized piece of paste with grape colour. Roll out thinly. Cut out the daisy shape. Cut out each petal individually and soften the edges with a ball tool. Curve slightly on a piece of foam. Attach to the cake surface.

10 Colour a small grape-sized piece of paste pale blue. Roll out thinly, cut out florets using a small plunger cutter. Remove the centre with a no. 2 piping tube. Glue in place. Paint on the stems and calyx with Christmas green. Dot each forget-me-not with a tangerine centre. Dust each rose centre with pale green. Define the edges of petals with dark pink dust. Pipe on the daisies using a no. 2 piping tube. Give each a warm yellow centre (melon with a touch of tangerine).

11 Using silk stamens, dust the tips brown and the cottons yellow. Cut them quite short. Pipe a bulb of pale yellow/green icing in the centre of the rose. Draw each stamen against the thumbnail to curve it. Insert into the icing with tweezers. Attach a pink bow to the bottom of the garland.

12 Pipe a snail trail around the base of the cake using a no. 2 piping tube. Add further buds and smaller flowers to fill any gaps. Attach the ribbons as shown in the photograph.

▶ *The rosebuds are made from two petals slightly overlapping.*

Julia's Rattle

This is a quick and easy cake, just right for beginners to attempt.

CAKE AND DECORATION

20cm (8 in) round fruit or Madeira cake · apricot glaze · 1kg (2 lb) marzipan (almond paste) 2kg (4 lb) sugarpaste · egg yolk, claret, grape, blueberry, chestnut and paste colours · gum arabic small amount of royal icing · 2m (2 yd) ribbon for rattle bow and board edge

EQUIPMENT

35 x 40cm (14 x 16 in) oblong cakeboard no. 2 crimper · animal-shaped biscuit (cookie) cutters · piping tube (tip) · round biscuit (cookie) cutter · small Garrett frill cutter

TIP
The technique used to decorate this cake is called crimping. It is an easy method which produces a professional finish and disguises poor surfaces such as cracks, indentations and air bubbles.

1 Cover the cakeboard with pale lemon sugarpaste. Allow it to dry. If the cake is too deep, cut a slice from the bottom. Carve the outer edge to make it domed. Cover the cake with marzipan then white sugarpaste. Place on the board in the top left-hand corner.

2 Colour 60g (2 oz) sugarpaste claret and grape and 30g (1 oz) in pale chestnut, egg yolk and blueberry.

3 Roll out a band of claret sugarpaste 5cm (2 in) wide. Make two lines of crimping using a no. 2 crimper. Trim close to the crimp line. Apply to the cake on a curve and angle as shown.

4 Roll out egg yolk or blueberry sugarpaste thinly. Cut out several animals and place them above and below the crimped band.

5 Roll out grape paste and crimp as before. Apply the chick motifs. Attach another line of animals above the former crimped band. For the top and bottom bands, roll out a band 2.5cm (1 in) wide. Cut out half-circles using the base of a piping tube.

6 For the very top of the rattle, cut out a circular scalloped shape using a small Garrett frill cutter but do not remove the centre. Simply lay half the shape over the remaining area and cut away the excess.

7 For the handle, form the sugarpaste into a long roll, wide at the top, near the cake, and gradually tapering towards the bottom. Cut the wide end and shape it with a large round biscuit cutter to make it butt against the circular cake. Attach a thin roll of paste around the join. Attach another for the circular base of the handle. Cut the ends of the roll straight, form a circle and butt together. Make another thin roll of paste and place over the join. Attach a ribbon to this join.

8 Choose some appropriate lettering (see page 9), make a template if necessary and pipe on the name of the baby. Finish the handle by piping small bulbs around the middle line of the hoop.

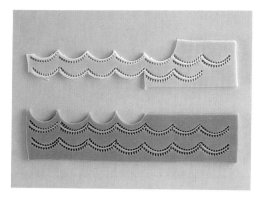

▲ *Make two lines of crimping, trim close to the crimp line and attach to the cake.*

Baby with Orchids

This cake uses a variety of techniques and is quite time-consuming. The curved spray of flowers reinforces the curved shape of the baby.

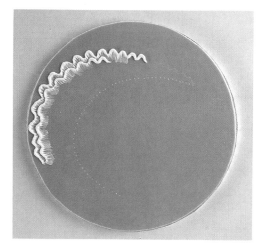

▲ *Pipe over the scribed scallops then brush downwards with a damp paintbrush.*

CAKE AND DECORATION

20cm (8 in) round fruit cake · apricot glaze
1kg (2 lb) marzipan (almond paste) · 1kg (2 lb)
sugarpaste · gum arabic · assorted paste and food
colourings · small amount of royal icing
60g (2 oz) modelling paste (bas relief paste)
assorted dusting powders (petal dust/blossom
tint) · butterfly cutter · 1m (1 yd) ribbon for
board edge

EQUIPMENT

28cm (11 in) round cakeboard · scriber · no. 4 and
no. 7 crimpers · piece of lace · ball tools · anger
tool · paintbrushes · piping tubes (tips) · cotton
26-gauge wire · dowelling or lace tool · pieces of
foam sponge · templates (see page 79)

1 Colour the sugarpaste a pale grape colour. Cover the cake with marzipan, then sugarpaste. When dry, scribe the frills of the pillow onto the sugarpaste. Using royal icing, pipe a line over the scribed scalloped shape as shown. Vary the pressure on the icing bag so that the icing is thinner at the base of the frill. Brush the icing with a damp paintbrush in downward strokes. Make a second line of frills and allow to dry.

2 Using template A, cut out a section of sugarpaste to act as a base on which to place the pillow and baby. Use template B to cut out the curved section from sugarpaste. Crimp the outer edge with a no. 7 crimper.

3 Use a piece of real lace to indent the next row of shapes. The bottom curved edge of lace has been emphasized with a no. 4 crimper. Use a scalpel to cut away the excess. Attach the finished piece of paste below the brush embroidery scallops.

▲ *Cut out a white base for the baby. Add more lace effect using crimpers.*

▲ *Use a piece of real lace held against card to indent the next row of shapes.*

4 Take a piece of sugarpaste, roll it into a ball and flatten to form the pillow. Smooth into shape using the traced pattern as a guide. Indent the pillow for the baby's head and body.

5 Colour some modelling paste flesh colour using paprika and a touch of melon. Place some silicone paper over the image of the baby's head and push the paste gently until it compares with the drawing. Indent a shape for the eye with an anger tool. Shape the eye socket using a very small ball tool. This will push some excess paste outwards which can be formed into a nose. Again with an anger tool, indent a line for the mouth.

6 Make a mark in which to place the ear. Indent to form the neck and chin. For the ear, take a small ball of paste and flatten it. (It is helpful to look at someone's ear when modelling the shape as it is quite complex.) Using the anger tool, push the top edge of the ear against the thumb to form a ridge.

Flatten the bottom edge for the lobe. Place the ear against the head and using the anger tool push the hole in the ear into the head to give a natural effect.

7 Using sugarpaste, form a crude body shape and blend the narrow upper part into the neck. Indent the area where the arm is to be placed. Mark the back of the yoke of the nightdress with the point of the anger tool to form pleats. Bend for the bottom and also for the area behind the knees.

8 Using a suitable colour for the hair, pipe some royal icing onto the head. Brush with a stiffened paintbrush (one that has been used to apply gum arabic is appropriate), to create a realistic hairstyle.

9 Cut out the coverlet from modelling paste using template C. Soften the cut edge with a ball tool and drape over the body. Create folds and pleats.

10 Shape an arm out of sugarpaste, bend and mould on the baby until the correct position and length is achieved. Use an anger tool to indent folds and pleats in the crook of the arm and shoulder. Open up the cuff area and place inside a small triangle of

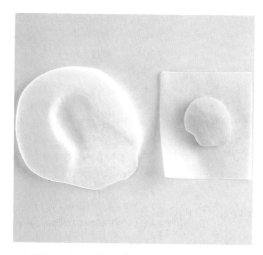

▲ *Form the pillow from a flattened ball of white paste and indent for the baby's head.*

◄ *Indent the area where the arm will rest. Mark pleats on the back of the nightdress.*

▼ *Paint lines and dots on the butterfly's wings and add some subtle shadowing.*

flesh-coloured paste for the hand. Press an anger tool along the top edge of the hand to form the knuckles.

11 Cut out the butterfly using a commercially made cutter. Soften the edges with a ball tool. Paint the wings using diluted paste colour and a fine brush. Dust the finished wings with petal dust to give a natural effect.

12 Using royal icing and no. 2 piping tube, colour the icing to enhance the butterfly. Pipe a bulb on the head. Apply more pressure to cover the thorax and more pressure again for the abdomen. Insert cotton stiffened with sugar syrup for antennae.

13 For the orchids, form a small ball of paste into an elongated hollow cone. Put in a 26-gauge wire at an angle. Slightly bend the paste to form a curve. Allow to dry. Cut out

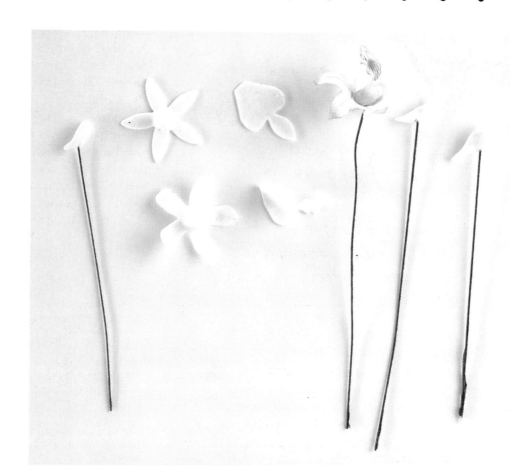

▶ *Fit the orchid petals around the cone-like shape. Allow to dry before painting.*

▼ *A small spray of orchids can also be added to the cake side, if wished.*

shape A. Soften the edges with a large ball tool and frill the tongue with a small ball tool. Cut the two side areas by balling inside the inner edge. Glue the cupped edges to the dried cone-like shape. Pull down the tongue and allow to dry.

14 Make a Mexican hat by forming a cone and flattening the bottom edge. Thin the edge still further with a small piece of dowelling or lace tool. Place cutter B over the cone and cut as shown. Open up the centre and ball and soften the edges. Place the shape on foam and curve each petal by placing a ball tool on the tip and drawing inwards towards the cone. Curl four petals in this way and reverse the curve for the fifth by turning the shape over. Insert the wire below the centre hole and between two petals. Pull the point of the first shape into the centre hole so that it fits firmly. Dust with green and cerise colour as shown.

15 Make spear-like leaves. Mark the lines with the anger tool. Soften the edges to create movement. Glue one end and wrap around the curves. Shape as necessary for a natural look.

Tumbling Teddies

The antics of these tumbling teddies will prove a talking point at any christening party. Try giving each one a different expression!

CAKE AND DECORATION
20cm (8 in) round cake · apricot glaze
1.25kg (2½ lb) marzipan (almond paste)
1.25kg (2½ lb) sugarpaste · 750g (1½ lb) royal
icing made with albumen (see page 5) · assorted
paste colours and dusting powders (petal dust/
blossom tint) · 1.5m (1½ yd) narrow ribbon
1m (1 yd) ribbon for board edge

EQUIPMENT
28cm (11 in) round cakeboard · piping tubes (tips)
tracing paper · silicone parchment · cranked
palette knife · perspex or glass · paintbrushes
templates (see page 24)

1 Cover the cake with marzipan, then sugarpaste. Cover the board with sugarpaste and allow to dry. Transfer the cake to the board and attach with a little royal icing. Pipe a snail trail around the base of the cake with a no. 2 piping tube.

2 Draw each teddy on a piece of tracing paper. You will need eight for the side of the cake, so repeat two designs. Place on the side of the tin used to bake the cake so that the resulting run-out will dry into a curved

shape to fit snugly to the cake side. Attach each corner of the drawing with double-sided tape. Place a piece of silicone parchment over the drawings.

3 Colour the royal icing with tartrazine-free cream paste colours, a little dark brown and a little chestnut. Outline each teddy with a no. 1 piping tube and stiff peak icing. Let down the icing with a little water until it is the right consistency. Draw the knife through the icing and count to ten – the

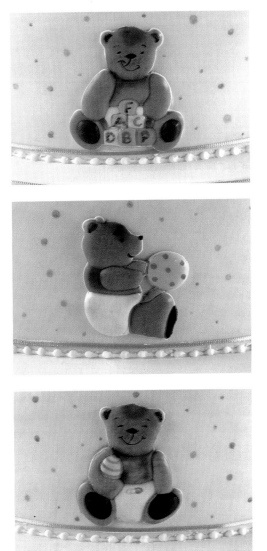

▲ *Make each teddy different by changing the activity and facial expression.*

23

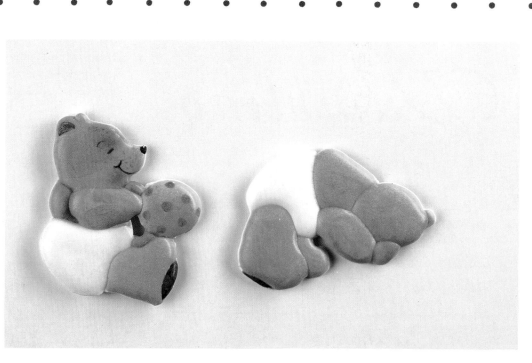

icing should find its own level within this time.

4 Fill a piping bag with icing; cut a tiny piece of paper from the point of the bag. Flood the areas furthest away, using a fine brush to help the icing into small corners. Leave the run-outs to dry on a piece of glass or perspex. Gently tap on the table top to help the icing find its own level, if necessary. Dry each part under a lamp for a shiny finish. Gradually work forward, to complete each teddy.

5 When dry, paint on details such as facial features and nappy pins using a fine brush. Dust shadows on the bears and their nappies. Remove the teddies from the paper with a cranked palette knife. Attach eight to the side of the cake with royal icing. Complete the teddy on top of the cake in same way, but dry it flat. Attach it to the top of the cake.

6 Run out the small toys and place around the train. Choose some appropriate lettering (see page 9), make a template if necessary and pipe on the name of the baby. Place a narrow ribbon above and below the teddies to create a

▲ *Drying the teddies under a lamp gives an attractive shiny finish.*

border all around the side of the cake. Paint on coloured circles in assorted sizes between the teddies. Attach ribbon around the board edge.

Enlarge by 154% on a photocopier

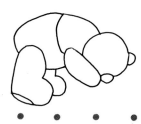

Megan

This beautiful hexagonal cake looks like it has been lifted straight out of the pages of a children's story book. With its intricate painting it is not a cake for beginners!

CAKE AND DECORATION

20cm (8 in) hexagonal cake · apricot glaze
1kg (2 lb) marzipan (almond paste)
1kg (2 lb) sugarpaste · assorted food colourings
and dusting powders (petal dust/blossom tint)
90g (3 oz) modelling paste (bas relief paste) · small
amount of royal icing · Garrett frill paste (see
page 8) · 1m (1 yd) picot-edged ribbon for
board edge

EQUIPMENT

28cm (11 in) cakeboard · scriber · anger tool
silicone parchment · doll's head mould · ball tool
assorted paintbrushes · blossom plunger cutters
single rose petal plunger cutter · heart-shaped
cutter · silk stamens · cocktail stick (toothpick)
Garrett frill cutter · piping tubes (tips) · pieces of
foam sponge · templates (see pages 28-32)

1 Cover the cakeboard with white sugarpaste and allow it to dry. Cover the cake with marzipan then sugarpaste. When dry, scribe the outline of the pillow and bed onto the cake.

2 Add a very small amount of apricot food colouring to a grape-sized piece of modelling paste. Roll out the paste fairly thickly and, using the pattern, cut out the shape of the pillow. Smooth all the cut edges with the

fingers, tweak out the corners and indent an area in which to place the head. Repeat for the mattress.

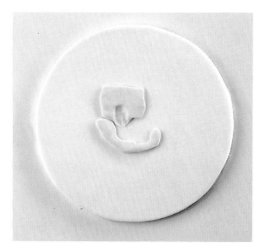

▲ *Cut out the pillow, smooth the edges and indent. Repeat for the mattress.*

3 Shape the inner edge of the mattress with an anger tool to create a rounded effect so that the coverlet will sit neatly upon it. Take a large grape-sized piece of paste and add a little more apricot colour to create a deeper shade. Place a piece of silicone parchment over the drawn image of the coverlet. Roll the paste into a ball and flatten between the heels of the hands

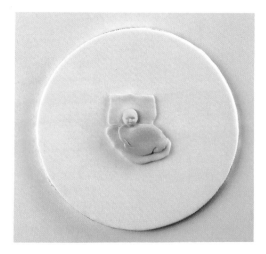

▲ *When the coverlet is in position, make folds with an anger tool, then add the head.*

so that the paste becomes rounded. Place on silicone parchment and push the paste gently with the fingers until it compares with the drawing. The edge of the coverlet should be at its thinest where it meets the pillow. Use an anger tool to indent creases and wrinkles.

4 For the head and hands, colour a small amount of paste paprika with a tiny amount of melon added. Make a head using a tiny doll's head mould (see page 9). Form the hands (see page 9) and place in a natural position as shown. Glue the head in place. Roll out a thin piece of white paste, cut out the sheet using the pattern and soften the edges with a ball tool. Fold under the top and bottom edges. Tuck under the baby's chin using an anger tool to indent for creases and folds.

5 For the painted background use Christmas green and gooseberry food colours. Keep the brush fairly dry as too much water will melt the sugar. Paint on the grass area, adding depth by varying the tone of the greens. Paint in leaves and fronds. Create a more 3D effect by adding further leaves and flowers using plunger cutters. For the leaves, cut out using the tiny single rose petal plunger cutter. Place the leaf on a piece of foam. Indent a vein line using the back of a scalpel. Apply to the cake so that the leaf sits up from the surface of the cake.

6 For the daisies, use a medium-size plunger cutter. Divide each petal in half. Roll a cocktail stick on each cut petal. Place on foam and rotate a small ball tool in the centre of the daisy to cup it.

7 For the toadstools, add a little dark brown to the paprika paste. Cut out the stalk and underneath part as one piece. Make a line with an anger tool for the upper edge of the stalk. Cut tiny lines for the gills. Make a dark red using a red compound colour. Cut out the toadstool cap, attach to the base and lift the bottom edge of the cap, so that it sticks up slightly. Use an anger tool on the upper edges to create a rounded look. Indent the top of the larger toadstool with a small ball tool so that the bird can sit neatly on it.

8 For the bird, cut out both wings as one from modelling paste. Use a scalpel to cut small V's for the feathers on each wing. Make a tiny ball in pale yellow paste for the stomach between the wings. Make another ball for the head and glue in place. Make a tiny hole for the beak. Make a tiny sausage tapered at each end, fold in half and place in the hole for the beak. For the tufts of grass, colour a small amount of paste with gooseberry food colour. Roll out thinly and cut out the grass sections.

Top design (Actual size)

Apply to the painted area and base of the toadstools.

9 Apply a frill on the pillow and mattress. Paint apricot spots onto the mattress. Paint the eyebrows, eyes and mouth on the baby and dust the cheeks. Pipe in the flower centres. Cut out two little chicks in yellow paste as shown. Use a template to scribe a line where each scene is to be placed on the six sides of the hexagon and proceed to work as above.

10 When the sides are complete, apply a Garrett frill (see page 8) onto the scribed line, thus framing the scene. Apply tiny dots of icing along the top edge of the frill with a no. 0 tube.

11 Make the butterflies with a small heart-shaped cutter. Cut out two hearts for each butterfly. Soften the edges with a ball tool. When dry, paint on the fine linear pattern in blue. Dust in pale blue all over the wings then dust the edges using a darker blue petal dust. Pipe the body using dark brown royal icing. For the head, thorax and abdomen, place the wings in each side of the thorax and support with small pieces of foam. Insert two tiny silk stamens. Attach to the top of each curve of the Garrett frill. Choose some appropriate lettering (see page 9), make a template if necessary and pipe the name of the baby. Attach the ribbon.

▲ *Paint on the background, then attach the leaves and flowers for a 3D effect.*

Actual size

Each of the six panels of the hexagon depicts a different woodland scene.

Panel 1

Panel 2

Actual size

Actual size

Panel 3

Panel 4

Actual size

Actual size

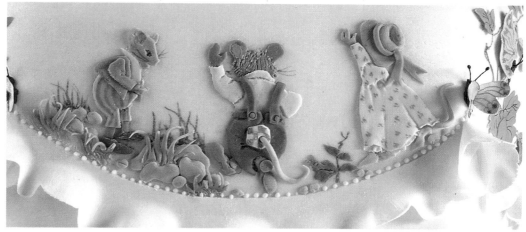

Panel 5

Panel 6

Actual size

Rock-a-Bye Baby

Inspired by a well-known nursery rhyme, this pretty cake would do equally well for a girl or a boy.

CAKE AND DECORATION
20cm (8 in) oval cake · apricot glaze
1kg (2 lb) marzipan (almond paste) · 1.25kg
(2½ lb) sugarpaste · 125g (4 oz) flower paste
mixed with 250g (8 oz) sugarpaste, coloured
brown, for basket base of cake · 60g (2 oz)
modelling paste (bas relief paste) · gum arabic
assorted paste colours · Garrett frill paste (see
page 8) · 30g (1 oz) royal icing · piping gel
1m (1 yd) narrow ribbon · 1m (1 yd) ribbon for
board edge

EQUIPMENT
28cm (11 in) oval cakeboard · scriber · basket-
weave rolling pin · anger tool · small blossom
plunger cutters · carnation cutter · piping tubes
(tips) · paintbrush · cocktail stick (toothpick)
28-gauge wire · pieces of foam sponge · template
(see page 34)

1 Cover the cake with marzipan, then sugarpaste. Measure around the cake using a strip of paper. Fold the paper into six equal sections and cut into the shape shown. Place the pattern around the cake and scribe a line around the top edge to denote the area for the basket-weave paste.

2 Taking the brown-coloured flower paste and sugarpaste mixture, roll into a long sausage. Press firmly with the textured roller, keeping the pressure consistent for the entire length. Lay the pattern shape over the paste and cut around it with a scalpel. Bring the cake down to the level of the paste. Wet the area where the basket weave is to be placed. Carefully attach the strip to the cake so that it does not stretch. Press lightly so that the basket weave is not damaged.

3 Scribe the image of the pillow, blanket and basket onto the cake surface. Take a walnut-sized piece of paste and round and flatten it into the pillow shape. Following the shape on the pattern, indent a place for the baby's head. Create creases in the pillow with an anger tool. Using the basket-coloured paste, cut out the inside edge of the basket near the bottom edge of the blanket.

4 Make the head of the baby from modelling paste coloured with paprika and a touch of melon, either using a mould (see page 9) or by rolling a grape-sized piece of paste. Cut the back of the head away so that it will nestle well into the pillow. Indent the closed eyes with an anger tool and make the nostrils using a cocktail stick. Open

▲ *The brown textured paste is used on the cake sides as well as for the baby's basket.*

Enlarge by
154% on a
photocopier

by adding extra white modelling paste.
Roll out fairly thinly and use the
textured roller to achieve the basket
weave, then cut out the basket using
the pattern. Glue down the bottom
curved edge. Open the upper area and
support with foam until dry. Roll a fine
rope of paste and attach it to the
surface of the cake. Mark with a scalpel
to create a twisted effect.

7 When the basket side is dry the
outer handle can be made. Push
some paste onto a 28-gauge wire and
roll until the paste is a similar thickness
to the inner handle. Curve until the
handle looks right. Mix a little of the
paste with the gum arabic until it is a
sticky consistency. Place a small
amount on the top of the handle
already on the cake and some more on
the upper edge of the outer handle.
Place the handle onto the glue at the
top of the inner handle (do not
penetrate the cake surface), then place
the lower end of the outer handle
underneath the top edge of the basket
side. Support in place if necessary.

the mouth using a scalpel. Make a little
ear (see page 20).

5 Make a blanket using a walnut-
sized piece of sugarpaste. Flatten
and shape it, round off the bottom
edge. Smooth it into the pattern shape.

6 For the basket, lighten the
colour of the paste used on the side

▶ *The outer
handle is
strengthened with
wire so that it can
be curved into
shape.*

8 When the handle is dry and firm, finish off the top edge of the basket with similar edging to that on the handle. Mix a little flower paste with sugarpaste and make a frill for the pillow and the bottom edge of the blanket using a carnation flower cutter. The frill can be enhanced by making holes using a no. 1 piping tube to give the appearance of lace. Make an extra-narrow strip to go across the blanket 1cm (½ in) below the top edge; this represents the edge of the top sheet.

9 Paint the lower part of the blanket with pale blue spots. Paint the eyelashes and eyebrows on the baby. Tint the mouth. Pipe on some blonde/brown hair with a no. 1 tube. Pipe the branches surrounding the basket with brown royal icing. Paint on some leaves using spruce and gooseberry green paste colours.

10 Colour some royal icing with Christmas green. Add a little piping gel so that the icing will dry more slowly. Using a no. 1 piping tube pipe in the tip and edges of leaves. With a no. 1 paintbrush, brush the icing towards the centre of the leaf and

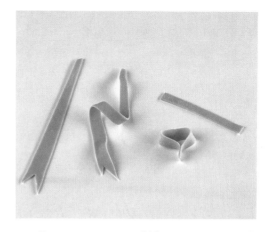

▲ *Cut narrow strips of blue sugarpaste and twist to represent ribbon.*

gradually work down the leaf. Add some small flowers and buds. Cut out some strips of blue sugarpaste to represent ribbon, or use real ribbon if preferred. Attach it at the top of the basket, twisting the ties around the handle as shown. Choose some appropriate lettering (see page 9), make a template if necessary and pipe on the name of the baby. Flood ice the two bluebirds, paint when dry and finally apply the Garrett frills around the cake (see page 8).

▼ *Apply the frills around the sides of the cake and finish with tiny bulbs of icing.*

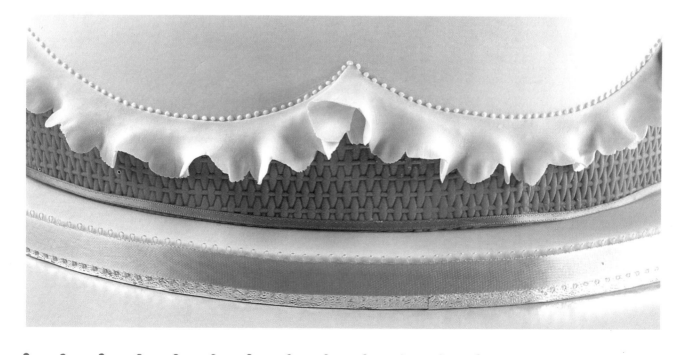

Frilled Cradle

*The charm of this cake lies in the delicacy of
the rows of Garrett frills and the precision
of the paintwork.*

CAKE AND DECORATION

20cm (8 in) square cake · apricot glaze
1kg (2 lb) marzipan (almond paste) · 1kg (2 lb)
sugarpaste · small amount of royal icing · claret,
paprika and melon food colourings · 60g (2 oz)
modelling paste (bas relief paste) · gum arabic
Garrett frill paste (see page 8) · 0.5m (½ yd)
narrow ribbon for cradle bow 1m (1 yd) ribbon for
board edge

EQUIPMENT

28cm (11 in) square cakeboard · piping tubes (tips)
scriber · doll's head mould · cocktail stick
(toothpick) · Garrett frill cutter · alphabet cutters
templates (see page 74)

1 Cover the cake with marzipan, then sugarpaste. Pipe a snail trail around the base of the cake using a no. 2 piping tube.

2 Trace the templates of the cradle, pillow and blanket. Place these shapes on the top of the cake and scribe a mark around them. Use a grape-sized piece of sugarpaste and form the pillow by pinching, flattening and pushing the paste into shape, using a piece of tracing paper over the pattern as a guide.

3 Roll out some modelling paste very finely and wrap around the pillow. Leave one side open and curl the paste backwards using the fingers to give a natural effect. Attach the pillow in place and indent an area for the baby's head.

4 Make the baby's head by either using a doll's head mould (see page 9), or by modelling a small head. Remember that only the upper part of the face need be visible. Make two small indentations for the closed eyes and two nostrils with the end of a cocktail stick. Make a tiny ear (see *Baby with Orchids*, page 20) and place into the indented area.

5 Make the cradle by rolling out some sugarpaste 5mm (¼ in) deep. Cut out the shape using the pattern. Smooth the cut edge with the fingers until rounded and attach in place.

6 Colour two small grape-sized pieces of modelling paste in two pale shades of claret, one slightly darker than the other. To create the padded effect, roll a pea-sized piece of pale pink paste into a ball, flatten and curve slightly. Attach to the cake surface. Make another shape using the darker

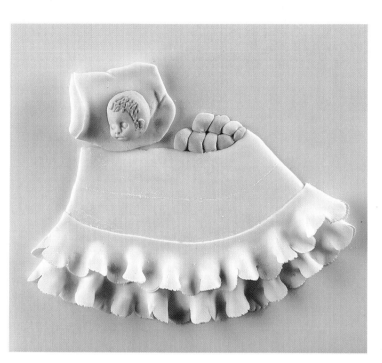

▲ *Roll balls of paste in two shades of pink, flatten slightly, then butt together.*

9 Pipe small dots of royal icing using a no. 1 piping tube on the top edge of the top frill. Colour some royal icing with light brown food colour and pipe hair onto the baby's head. Stamp out the word Congratulations using alphabet cutters (see page 9 for alternative methods of lettering).

▲ *Apply the frills in layers, graduating the shades from dark to light.*

pink and push into the previous shape; repeat using the paler colour. Continue until the blanket is complete. When dry, paint a tiny pattern on each square and fine pink lines on the side of the pillow.

7 Make a small Garrett frill (see page 8) and place around the base of the cradle. Gradually work up the cradle until complete. Make a tiny frill around the top of the cradle facing the opposite way. When dry, paint pink dots onto the frills. Finally, attach a piece of narrow ribbon onto the top seam between the final Garrett frill and the inward-facing frill with small dots of royal icing. Attach two tiny bows and two tails onto the ribbon.

8 Pipe a snail trail around the base of the cake. Colour some frilling paste three shades of pink. Attach the darkest pink to the base of the cake in each of the four corners and gradually work upwards. When all the pink frills have been attached, make one final frill all around the cake in white. When dry, paint tiny pink dots onto this frill to match the cradle.

▲ *Alphabet cutters were used on this cake; an easy alternative to piping.*

Cutwork Teddy

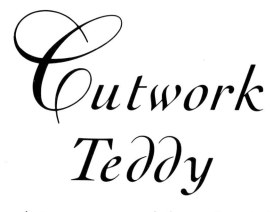

Cutwork is a very straightforward technique to master. All you have to do is make card templates for each colour on the image. Start with the background, then gradually work forward to build up the picture.

CAKE AND DECORATION
20cm (8 in) square cake · apricot glaze
1kg (2 lb) marzipan (almond paste) · 1kg (2 lb)
sugarpaste · 60g (2 oz) modelling paste (bas relief
paste) · assorted paste colours · assorted dusting
powders (petal dust/blossom tint) · 1m (1 yd)
3mm (⅛ in) blue and 1m (1 yd) 3mm (⅛ in)
apricot ribbon · 1m (1 yd) ribbon for board edge

EQUIPMENT
piping tube (tip) · assorted paintbrushes
template (see page 76)

---

1 Cover the cake with marzipan, then sugarpaste. Cut out the teddy's body in one piece and indent the shape of the chin, inner arms and stomach.

2 Cut out the ear using the base of a piping tube. Cut out the inner ear using a paler colour, again using the base of a piping tube. Smooth the edges with the fingers until the join is quite smooth. Continue to work in this way until the image is complete.

3 Finish off by painting on details such as the name, the patterns on the bow tie and the flag. When adding dusting powder, be aware that any colour added to paste that has already been coloured will not be pure; for example, yellow dusting powder added to blue paste will be slightly green. It is better therefore, if a high density of colour is needed, to cut out the shape from white paste.

4 For the ball and the handle of the box use a number of circular cutters to cut out the shapes then butt them together. To make the box handle, cut out two layers of paste so that the handle is on a level with the box. For the feeding bottle, dry the bottle shape before adding to the cap, so that it does not droop.

5 Complete the image by creating shadows on the bear using dusting powder around eyes, stitching, under the arms and so on.

6 Add the narrow ribbons to the side of the cake to complement the colours used in the main design. Finish with two neat bows.

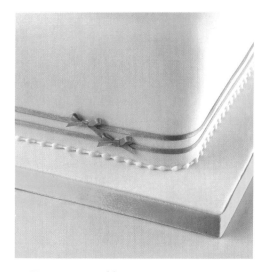

▲ *Two narrow ribbons in contrasting colours provide a smart and simple finish.*

Baby in Lace

Although this cake looks complicated, it is really quite straightforward. It is probably more suitable for a baby girl because of the heavily embroidered christening dress.

CAKE AND DECORATION

20cm (8 in) round cake · apricot glaze
1kg (2 lb) marzipan (almond paste) · 1.25kg
(2½ lb) sugarpaste · 60g (2 oz) modelling paste
(bas relief paste) · paprika, melon, claret and
blueberry paste colours · 90g (3 oz) royal icing
30g (1 oz) flower paste · gum arabic · 1m (1 yd)
narrow ribbon · 1m (1 yd) ribbon for board edge

EQUIPMENT

28cm (11 in) round cakeboard · ball tool · anger
tool · piping tubes (tips) · paintbrushes · assorted
heart cutters · miniature rose petal or broiderie
anglaise tool · dove mould · pieces of foam
sponge · templates (see page 76)

TIP
*The lace pattern
of the dress can
be varied and
could be modelled
on actual lace.
It is created by
using the petals
from various
flower cutters.*

1 Cover the cakeboard with white sugarpaste and allow to dry. Cover the cake with marzipan, then sugarpaste. Place the covered cake on the board. Roll a 60g (2 oz) piece of sugarpaste into a ball and flatten it between the hands. Attach to the top of the cake with gum arabic.

2 Taking a further 60g (2 oz) piece of paste, flatten as before, but also flatten the edges and tweak the four corners to form a square cushion. Place this second cushion onto the first. Flatten and carve away the corner of the first cushion so that this second cushion will sit more upright. Repeat this process again so that the third and final cushion will sit correctly.

3 For the final cushion, roll a 90g (3 oz) piece of paste between the palms of the hands and flatten as for the first cushion. Indent the area where the baby's head will be placed, as shown. For the baby's head, colour some modelling paste with a little paprika and a touch of melon. Roll a large grape-sized piece of paste into a ball (make sure there are no cracks or marks on the surface). Roll the little finger halfway down the paste as shown. Tweak out the nose and narrow it with the fingers. Indent a hole for each eye with a ball tool. Indent around the eye socket with the ball tool to finish off the eye shape.

4 For the mouth, use the flatter end of an anger tool and inset into the mouth. Mark the shape of the lips with the point of the tool. Mark the channel between the nose and the mouth, again with the tip of the tool. Use the tool to flatten the area below the jaw line. At the top of the jaw line place a small ear (see page 20). Glue in place with gum arabic.

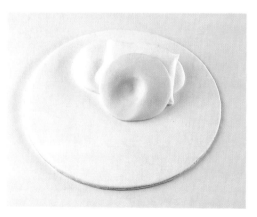

▲ *Assemble the three cushions then indent the area for the baby's head.*

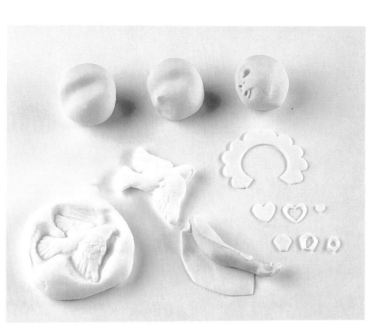

▲ *The build-up of the baby's head, the dove, the lace patterns and baby's arm.*

5 Place a small ball of white paste into the eye socket for the eyeball. When the eyeball has dried, attach a flat, elongated, triangular piece of flesh-coloured paste to the upper part of the eyeball to form the eyelid. Lift the paste away from the eyeball slightly so that it looks more natural.

6 Make a small hand with a wrist, (see page 9). Roll out a little white modelling paste. Place the hand onto the white paste and cut around the wrist area using the pattern. Ball the wrist edge to soften it, wrap the paste around the wrist with the paste on the underside. Flatten the end of the wrist and attach to the cake under the head. Lift the hand away from the cake surface and support with foam until dry.

7 Make a small bodice by moulding a large grape-sized piece of sugarpaste around the head. Indent a place for the arm to rest. Make a deep indentation for the shoulder socket so that the arm will lift well away from the bodice when attached. Make a whole arm.

8 Roll out some more white modelling paste, cut out the sleeve and soften the wrist edge. Wrap around the arm. Keep the seam on the underside. Trim away any excess paste, especially in the shoulder socket area.

9 Take 60g (2 oz) of sugarpaste, roll between the hands to form a cone, flatten and butt up against the bodice of the dress. Smooth the surface with the palm of the hand. Make pleats beneath the bodice with an anger tool.

10 Roll out 30g (1 oz) of modelling paste quite finely and cut out the dress using the pattern. Persuade the dress into the pleated area beneath the bodice. Arrange the dress in natural looking folds. Curve the side edges around the sugarpaste so that the material appears to wrap around the baby's main dress shape. When the dress is dry, roll out some white modelling or flower paste very finely. Cut out blossom and heart shapes of various sizes, using flower cutters to create a lace filigree pattern, and attach to the bottom edge of the dress. Complete the lace effect by outlining the shapes with dots of royal icing using a no. 0 piping tube. Repeat this process for a similar effect around the side of the cake.

11 To complete the cushions, add a small frill to the bottom one and a pale-blue strip of paste to the inside edge of the square one. Apply patterns to the cushions using a very fine paintbrush and diluted paste colours. Make sure the brush is fairly dry when applying the colour.

12 Colour a grape-sized piece of modelling paste pale claret. Roll out finely into a long strip. Cut out a 3mm x 3cm (1/8 x 1 1/4 in) piece of ribbon for the waist of the dress. Cut two tails and twist. Attach to the cake surface.

13 Colour some flower paste pale claret and make some miniature roses using a tiny petal plunger cutter or a single petal from a broiderie anglaise cutter. Arrange into a small

◄ *Make a deep vertical indentation on the bodice for the upper arm.*

▼ *Flower cutters are used for the lace on the dress, and on the cake sides.*

bouquet and decorate with a pink bow.

14 For the dove, take a 30g (1 oz) piece of sugarpaste, roll it between the palms of the hands until there are no creases, then flatten gently. Dust the dove mould and the sugarpaste with cornflour and press firmly into the mould. Trim away the excess paste and smooth the cut edges. Emphasize the eye with the tip of a no. 1 piping tube.

15 Allow the dove to dry, then apply a little glue, made by working a spot of gum arabic into a pea-sized piece of paste with a palette knife, behind the dove's beak. Curve the stem of one of the miniature roses and insert into the paste, support and leave to dry.

16 When the rose is quite secure, apply more of the sticky paste to the underside of the lower wing. Place the dove on the christening dress in the position shown and support until dry.

Adam's Bib

An unusual and original shape for a cake. The paintwork can be simplified if time or talent is in short supply!

CAKE AND DECORATION

28 x 23 x 5cm (11 x 9 x 2 in) slab Madeira or fruit cake · apricot glaze · 1kg (2 lb) marzipan (almond paste) · 1kg (2 lb) sugarpaste · 60g (2 oz) modelling paste (bas relief paste) · assorted food colourings · gum arabic · Garrett frill paste (see page 8) · 1m (1 yd) narrow ribbon · 1m (1 yd) ribbon for board edge

EQUIPMENT

35 x 30cm (14 x 12 in) oblong cakeboard assorted piping tubes (tips) · scriber · thin card assorted paintbrushes · blossom plunger cutters ball tool · heart-shaped cutter · alphabet cutters Garrett frill cutter · pieces of foam sponge template (see page 48)

1 Cover the cakeboard with sugarpaste and leave it to dry. Trim the cake to shape. Cover the cake with marzipan then sugarpaste and attach it to the board. Pipe a snail trail around the bottom of the cake with a no. 2 piping tube. Scribe the pattern on top of the cake.

2 Colour a grape-sized piece of sugarpaste pale lemon for the chicks. Make a template for the chicks from thin card. Roll the paste out thinly, cut around the card and attach the chicks to the surface of the cake with gum arabic. Smooth around the cut edge with a clean finger.

3 Cut out the parcel shapes in the chosen colours and attach as before. To make the balls, roll grape-pip size pieces of paste between the fingers, apply a dot of gum arabic to the cake, press each ball on and flatten with a finger.

4 Cut out the ribbons, sailing boats and bows and attach to the cake. When all the shapes are dry, paint on the stripes, spots and other patterns, and the blue ribbon linking all the elements together.

5 Make some tiny flowers using plunger cutters. Ball each one on foam and attach. Pipe in a centre or paint in a tiny dot of colour. Add miniature painted leaves to complete the design.

6 Add some small white hearts to give interest to the centre of the cake. Cut out the name using alphabet cutters and position at the neck of the bib (see page 9 for alternative methods of lettering).

7 Make a Garrett frill (see page 8) and attach to the sides of the cake. Finish off the frill by piping small dots of icing with a no. 0 piping tube.

▲ *The top of the Garrett frill is finished with dots of royal icing.*

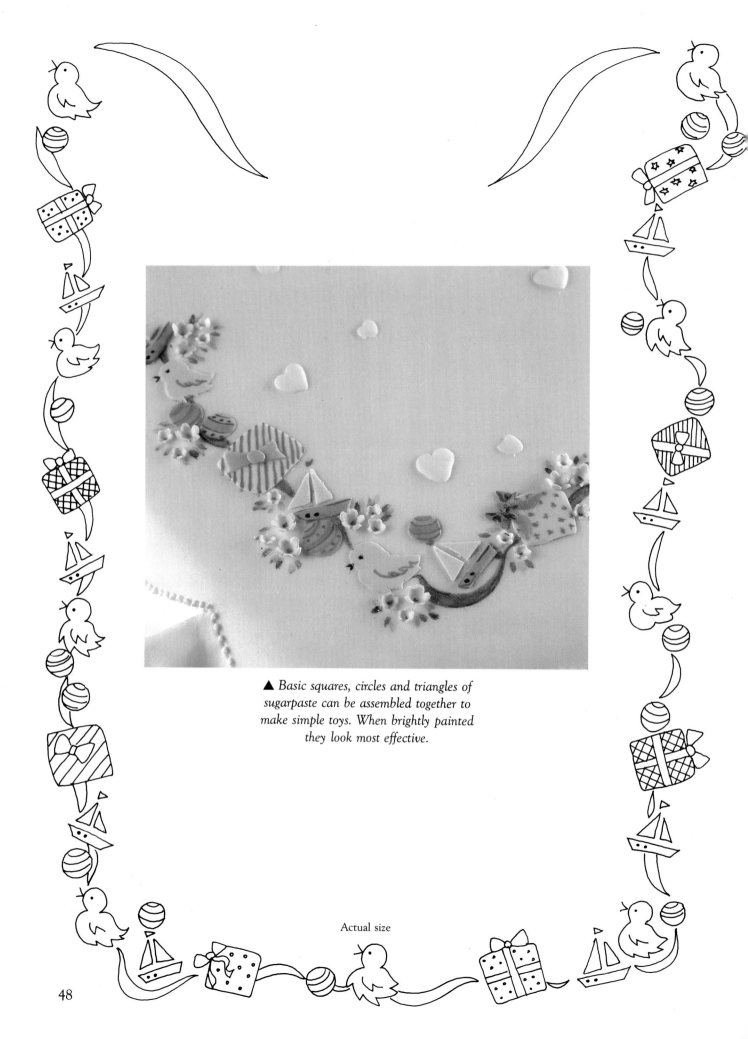

▲ *Basic squares, circles and triangles of sugarpaste can be assembled together to make simple toys. When brightly painted they look most effective.*

Actual size

A Cosy Chick

This charming cake need not be finished to the standard shown here – the quilt could be left unpainted, if wished, and just given some texture with absorbent kitchen paper.

CAKE AND DECORATION

20cm (8 in) round fruit cake · apricot glaze
1kg (2 lb) marzipan (almond paste) · 1kg (2 lb)
sugarpaste · blueberry, chestnut, dark brown,
melon, egg yolk, paprika and black paste colours
60g (2 oz) modelling paste (bas relief paste) · gum
arabic · assorted paste colours for painting the
quilt · 1m (1 yd) pink and 1m (1 yd) mauve narrow
ribbon · 1m (1 yd) ribbon for board edge

EQUIPMENT

28cm (11 in) round cakeboard · round plaque
cutter · gelatine plaque (see page 5) · scriber
medium heart cutter · fine paintbrushes · ball tool
anger tool · absorbent kitchen paper · templates
(see page 76)

---

1 Cover the cake with marzipan. Add some blueberry paste colour to the sugarpaste and knead for a short time so that when the paste is cut in half the effect is linear and streaky. Roll out the paste at this stage. If it is overworked the marbled effect will be lost. Cover the cake, then remove a disc of paste from the centre using a plaque or biscuit cutter. Cut out a plaque from

gelatine paste with the same cutter so that it will be the correct size. Allow the plaque to dry.

2 When dry, scribe the chick in bed image onto the plaque. Colour a small amount of modelling paste with a spot of chestnut and dark brown paste colour. Using the templates, cut out the shape for the bed head. Use a medium-sized heart cutter to stamp out a heart from the centre of the bed head. Glue in place with gum arabic.

▲ *Attach the brown paste bed head to the plaque. The wood effect is added later.*

3 Roll sugarpaste between the hands and tweak out the corners to form the pillow. The pillow should sit half way between the two end posts. If it is too large, trim away the excess and smooth the cut edge. Indent the area where the chick and teddy's head will lie. Allow it to dry. Paint one side of the pillow with pink stripes as shown. Using a piece of absorbent kitchen paper to make a template, wrap around the pillow so that one side of the pillow (where the pink stripes have been painted) is left open and the other two sides are covered. The bottom edge is hidden by the quilt, so leave flat.

4 Roll out some sugarpaste finely and using the template cut out the pillowcase. Ball the edge that will be left open so that it can be pushed back over the stripes to give the appearance of material. Persuade the paste gently into

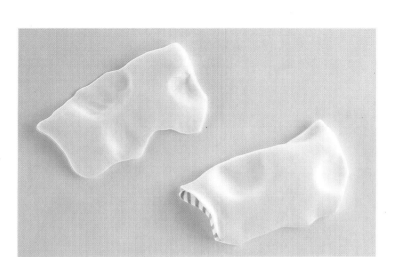

▲ *Paint one side of the pillow with candy stripes.*

▶ *The teddy's ears are two-tone cones; the chick's feathers marked on with a scalpel.*

for each cheek. Use a scalpel to mark on the feathered texture.

5 For the dummy, form a tiny sugar-paste pea and flatten it. Glue into the indented hole in the face. Make a tiny ball, inset an anger tool into each opposite side to form the central link. Place this in the middle of the flattened piece. Roll out a thin strand of paste and form it into a ring. Place one end of the ring into the side of the link.

6 For the teddy's head, use paprika paste to resemble fur colour. Add a little yellow to give a more golden appearance. Take a small piece of paste and form an oval. Use a ball tool to indent an oval hole for the muzzle and two smaller holes for the eyes.

7 Use a white pea-sized piece of paste to form an oval shape that will fit inside the indented muzzle. Use a scalpel to mark the central division below the nose and indent a small oval for the nose. Place in a black nose and two tiny black balls for the eyes.

the indented areas and glue into place. For the chick's head, colour a small amount of modelling paste with melon paste colour. Add a touch of egg yolk to warm up the colour. Roll it into a ball and flatten so that it is big enough to fill in the indented space. Use a ball tool to indent a hole in which to place the dummy. Cut a curve for each eye with a scalpel. Make a pea-sized ball of paste

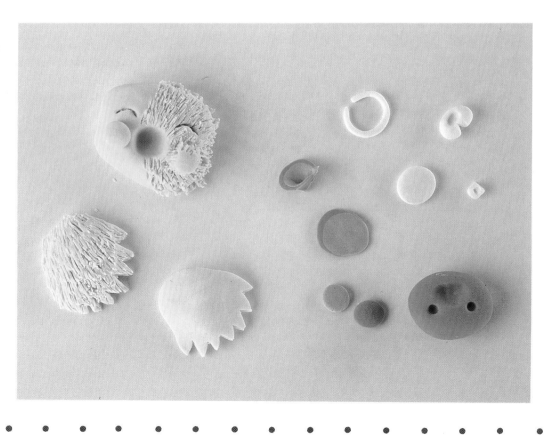

8 For the ears, take a small piece of the teddy-coloured paste and lighten it by adding some white. Make a small pea shape in each colour. Flatten with finger and thumb. Place the lighter colour slightly below the darker colour so that it forms an edge. Push the bottom edge of the ear together and cut away the excess paste at the back. Attach in place.

9 Use the wing template to roughly form the shape of the chick's wings from yellow paste. Cut away the bottom edge to form feathers and glue in place. Make the feather texture with the scalpel as for the head.

10 Use absorbent kitchen paper to make the template for the quilt. This will drape more easily over the two figures than stiff parchment. When the desired shape has been achieved, cut out the shape in parchment. Parchment will not make any marks on the sugarpaste when the quilt is cut out whereas the absorbent kitchen paper has a textured surface. This latter effect can be desirable, especially if you wish to leave the quilt unpainted. The quilt is cut out wider than necessary so that it can be draped into folds across the bed. Take time to achieve the desired effect. Allow it to dry. When dry, divide the quilt into squares and use a no. 1 paintbrush and assorted paste colours to paint the patchwork quilt with alternate boxes of stripes, spots, flowers and squares, as illustrated.

▼ *Drape the quilt into natural folds before painting. Add toys to the board, if wished.*

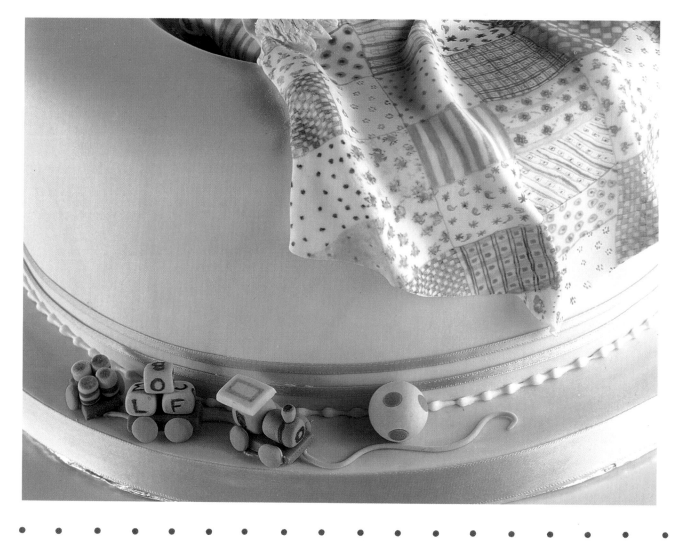

Painted Portrait

*The cocoa-painted image on this cake resembles
the old-fashioned sepia prints of the 1940s,
when photographs were hand-tinted.*

CAKE AND DECORATION
15cm (6 in) oval cake · apricot glaze · 750g
(1½ lb) marzipan (almond paste) · 750g (1½ lb)
sugarpaste · cocoa butter · cocoa powder · blue
paste colour · small amount of royal icing
Garrett frill paste (see page 8) · 1.25m (1¼ yd)
ribbon for cake and board edge

EQUIPMENT
23cm (9 in) oval cakeboard · gelatine plaque large
enough to accommodate picture (see page 5)
assorted paintbrushes · scriber · piping tubes
(tips) · Garrett frill cutter

TIP
*Start by taking a
black-and-white
photograph of the
baby – the tones
are easier to
follow than they
would be from
colour.*

1 Cover the cake with marzipan, then sugarpaste. Place the cake on the cakeboard. Make a plaque using gelatine paste and allow to dry thoroughly.

2 Either scribe the image onto the plaque or trace the outline using a fine-tipped brown pencil. Do not put in too much detail as the lines could show through the lighter tones of the cocoa butter and spoil the finished product.

3 Melt small amounts of butter in four small screw-topped glass jars by placing the jars in a shallow pan

of hot water. Add a little cocoa powder to the first jar, a little more to the second and so on until you have three distinct tones. In the final jar, make quite a concentrated mix for defining the eyes and any deep shadows.

4 To paint the image, first cover the baby and surrounding blanket and pillow in the palest tone. While still warm, continue to add the medium tone on the dress, blanket, fingers and features. Finally, add the darkest tones for eyes, nostrils, inner mouth and hair. Allow to dry.

5 Add a little blue paste colour to the brush to paint the blanket. Wipe the brush well with tissue before replacing it in the glass jar. When dry, use a scriber or fine scalpel to scratch

▲ *First cover the image with the palest tone
to create a colour-washed background.*

▲ *Build up the picture with the darker
tones, adding shadow and definition.*

▲ *Use the darkest tone for detail. Scratch off the cocoa to create highlights.*

into the cocoa to create highlights. This will bring life to the eyes and a natural look to the hair. When the design is complete, simply cover the jars of cocoa butter and store. To use again, replace the jars in hot water and stir

well as the cocoa tends to separate.

6 Roll out some sugarpaste 20mm (¾ in) thick. Cut out an oval using the plaque cutter. Attach to the top of the cake with a little water and allow to dry. Attach the cocoa-painted plaque with a little royal icing. Using a no. 2 piping tube pipe a snail trail around the base of the cake and the base of the plaque. Attach a Garrett frill (see page 8), around the base of the plaque in the normal position, and attach another frill above the first, facing upwards. When dry, attach the picot-edged ribbon between the two frills as shown. This gives an effect rather like a collar on top of the cake. Attach a matching piece of ribbon around the base of the cake.

◄ *Attach two Garrett frills back to back to make a collar that will frame the plaque.*

$\mathscr{A}$ Pair of Bootees

This cake needs to be kept fairly simple as the bootees are so large and elaborate.

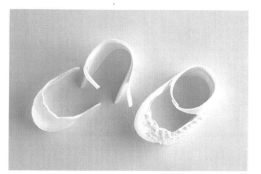

▲ *Cut the bootees from thick modelling paste. Glue the sections together.*

CAKE AND DECORATION

25 x 20cm (10 x 8 in) oval fruit cake · apricot glaze · 1kg (2 lb) marzipan (almond paste) 1kg (2 lb) sugarpaste · 90g (3 oz) modelling paste (bas relief paste) · gum arabic · 30g (1 oz) flower paste · melon food colouring · small amount of royal icing · Garrett frill paste (see page 8) · 25cm (10 in) narrow ribbon for bootee bows · 1m (1 yd) ribbon for board edge

EQUIPMENT

28cm (11 in) oval cakeboard · medium blossom plunger cutter · large ball tool · piping tube (tip) silicone parchment · Garrett frill cutter templates (see page 77)

TIP
The bootees can be made much smaller by reducing the pattern on a photocopier and decorating with a smaller blossom plunger cutter.

1 Cover the cake with marzipan, then sugarpaste. Each bootee consists of two parts; the heel with straps and the toe. Using the templates, cut out both sections from modelling paste rolled out fairly thickly so that it will support itself when standing upright. Place the heel section with the side pieces fairly straight and the straps overlapping. Glue the straps in place with gum arabic.

2 Cut out the front section. Use a large ball tool to shape the area within the dotted line for the toe. The front side sections should just slip over the back side sections. The bootee can be made as long or as short as required at this stage. Glue the sections together and leave to set.

3 For the second bootee, repeat as before, but when making the front remember to reverse the template.

4 Using a blossom plunger cutter stamp out dozens of small flowers and allow them to dry. Attach to the bootees with royal icing. Place a small bow at the centre of each strap. Attach the bootees to the top of the cake by piping small dots of royal icing around the edge of the soles.

5 Finally, pipe dots of royal icing all round the visible upper edge of each bootee. Choose some appropriate lettering (see page 9), make a template if necessary and pipe on the name of the baby. Attach Garrett frills to the side of the cake (see page 8), finishing with dots of royal icing and more flowers.

▲ *Pipe dots of royal icing and attach more flowers around the top of the frills.*

Joy

This beautiful cake will appeal to lovers of elegance and tradition. It is equally suitable for a baby girl or boy's christening.

CAKE AND DECORATION
23cm (9 in) oval fruit cake · apricot glaze · 1.25kg (2½ lb) marzipan (almond paste) · 1.25kg (2½ lb) sugarpaste · 60g (2 oz) modelling paste (bas relief paste) · small amount of royal icing · Garrett frill paste (see page 8) · grape, paprika, melon and blueberry food colourings · pink and blue dusting powders (petal dust/blossom tint) · black food pen · 1m (1 yd) ribbon for board edge

EQUIPMENT
28cm (11 in) oval cakeboard · scriber · silicone parchment · ball tool · piping tubes (tips) Garrett frill cutter · soft paintbrushes · pieces of foam sponge · templates (see page 77)

1 Cover the cake with marzipan, then white sugarpaste. When the sugarpaste is dry, scribe the image of the baby onto the cake.

2 Colour a small amount of modelling paste with grape food colouring, then cut out the back of the hood. When in position, soften and flatten the edges. Make a sausage shape in the same colour. Taper each end to a fine point and curve into the correct size and shape using the pattern as a guide. Pinch the top edge until it is quite fine, as shown. Attach in place.

▲ *Pinch the top edge of the hood until it is quite fine, then attach it.*

3 Take a large grape-size piece of paste, again in the pale grape colour. Flatten and round to form the pillow. Indent the area for the baby's head. Colour another grape-sized piece of paste flesh colour, using a touch of paprika and an even smaller touch of melon. Form the shape into a ball, flatten and indent the area between the eyebrow and the cheek. Place onto the pillow. Make a small ear (see *Baby with Orchids*, page 20), and attach in place.

4 Using 15g (½ oz) sugarpaste, create the rough shape of the body, following the pattern. Using modelling paste, cut out the dress sections. Ball

▲ *Place the baby's head on the pillow, then make and attach a small ear.*

▶ *Ball the edges of the dress, turn, then support the edges with foam.*

the side that needs to be frilled and fold so that the edges become fine. Butt the first dress shape against the sugarpaste body. Fold back the outer edge and lift the edges to form pleats.

5 Attach the main dress shape over entire body. Turn the bottom edge and lift to create movement. Cut out and attach pattern shape A to the side edge of the dress. Again, ball the edges and support the curves with small pieces of foam. Continue to work over the entire dress using the pattern pieces provided and, following the main diagram, pipe on the hair with royal icing. Pipe a small curved eyelash. Paint on a fine eyebrow and dust a little colour onto the cheek.

6 Scribe the outer line of the window onto the cake, slightly inside the pattern line. Using a food pen, draw on the latticed line. Allow to dry. Colour with blue, lilac and pink dusting powders. Colour the dress, hood etc, on the baby. Use the dusting powder in a darker shade inside the hood and under the deeper folds of the dress. Lighten the colour with cornflour for the paler shades.

7 Use the pattern for the window. Pipe the outline onto waxed paper or plastic wrap placed over the pattern with a no. 1 piping tube. Carefully flood the area between the piped lines with a softer icing in the numbered order so that the sills stand out clearly to give a

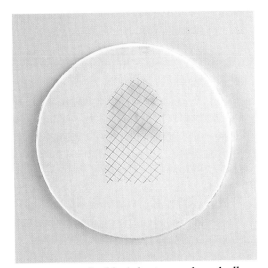

▲ *Draw on the black lattice-work and allow to dry before applying dusting powder.*

3D effect. Persuade the icing into the corners using a fine brush. When complete, dry under a lamp. This will give the surface a slight sheen. The name of the child can be created in the same way.

8 Complete the cake by applying a Garrett frill (see page 8). To make sure the frills are of equal length, wrap a piece of silicone parchment 7.5cm (3 in) deep around the side of the cake. Cut the paper so that both ends butt together. Fold the paper into the number of frills that are required. Fold the paper in half and draw on the shape of the frill as illustrated below. Open up

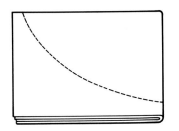

the pattern, wrap around the side of the cake and secure with masking tape, then scribe the frill around the cake. Remove the paper.

Actual size

9 Moisten below the scribed line with water and attach the frill. Raise the frill with the tail-end of a paintbrush to even up the folds and give lift where needed.

10 When adding the second frill allow some excess paste at the top edge so that this can be turned under to form a natural fold. Neaten by piping small dots of royal icing along the upper edge of the frill. When the frill is dry and firm, dust the edge with lilac or pink. Pipe a snail trail around the base of the cake.

Teddy with Daisies

Much can be made of the varying textures found on this cheeky teddy; his thick brown fur and soft terrycloth nappy contrast beautifully with the smooth white sugarpaste background.

CAKE AND DECORATION
20cm (8 in) round cake · apricot glaze
1kg (2 lb) marzipan (almond paste) · 1kg (2 lb)
sugarpaste · 90g (3 oz) modelling paste (bas relief
paste) · 125g (4 oz) flower paste · cream, chestnut,
dark brown, grape, black and silver food
colourings · yellow, cream and pink dusting
powders (petal dust/blossom tint) · gum arabic
1m (1 yd) narrow picot-edged ribbon · 1m (1 yd)
ribbon for board edge

EQUIPMENT
28cm (11 in) round cakeboard · scriber · assorted
paintbrushes · piping tubes (tips) · tweezers
veiner · ball tool · gelatine crystals · 28- and 26-
gauge wire · cocktail stick (toothpick) · snowdrop
cutter · heart-shaped cutter · stemwrap · pieces of
foam sponge · template (see page 77)

TIP
For a simpler version, leave off the flowers and position the teddy centrally.

1 Cover the cake with marzipan then sugarpaste. Scribe the shape of the teddy onto the cake. Complete all the background shapes first then work gradually forwards. First make the arms, then the tummy, the nappy, the head and finally the feet.

2 Colour the paste to be used for the teddy with some cream food colour with a little chestnut, dark brown and black added. Cut out the shape of the arm and attach to the cake surface. With a sharp scalpel, mark the surface of the paste to give an impression of fur. Work in the direction the fur should grow. Repeat for the second arm.

3 Roll out some paste a little more thickly for the stomach and attach, marking as before. Make a seam down the centre of the body. Roll out some white sugarpaste and attach to the nappy area. Pinch with the tips of tweezers to give a towelling effect.

4 To make the nappy pin roll out a pea-sized piece of pale blue modelling paste. Cut out the metal top using the template. Remove the hole in the middle using a no. 3 piping tube. Indent a line from the hole to the bottom edge using a veining tool. Roll out a very thin white roll of paste. Cut two 1cm (½ in) sections, flatten one end of each and attach under the blue metal section. Twist the remaining roll as shown overleaf to form the bottom of the safety pin. When dry, paint with silver food colour. Push both sections into the nappy and lay a small strip of

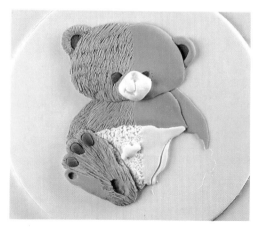

▲ *Mark the paste to resemble fur. Vary the direction of growth for each body part.*

white paste over the middle of the pin. Work in some texture with the tweezers so that the edges blend in with the nappy.

5 Cut out the shape of the head a little more thickly than the stomach and attach in place. Mark as before. Indent the shape for the eyes. Attach a piece of white modelling paste for the muzzle. Indent an area for the nose and mark in the mouth. Cut out and position the tongue, curling the end to give a natural look.

6 Cut out the inner ear shape in deep chestnut brown. Make a small roll, curve and place around the inner ear. Texture as before.

7 Cut out the feet quite thickly. Indent for the pad areas. Use deep chestnut paste for the pads, roll them into shape using the template as a guide and place into the indentations to give a rounded effect. Texture the surface of the feet, again, bearing in mind the shape and the direction of the fur. When dry, dust between the toes on the seam lines and between the arms and stomach to create depth.

8 Add the eyes using deep chestnut paste, paint in the pupil, and glaze when the eyes are dry. Make a small triangular nose with a tiny piece of black paste and indent two nostrils.

9 Colour a grape-sized piece of paste with a little blue food colour. Roll out quite finely. Make small balls of pale pink paste and press on top. When all the balls have been attached, roll over once with a small rolling pin. Cut out two sections of the tie. Soften the edges with a ball tool and fold A to B. Create creases and folds to form a natural look. Place a flattened ball of paste between both loops.

10 To make a crescent-shaped spray of wild flowers; start by forming the centre of the daisy. Roll a pea-sized piece of paste into a ball and flatten into a stubby cone. Pull a hooked 26-gauge wire into the paste. Plug the hole that is formed with a tiny ball of paste, flatten and allow to dry. When dry, coat the top of the cone with gum arabic then place the wet cone into a jar containing gelatine crystals coloured with yellow dusting powder.

11 Roll out some white flower paste thinly and cut out the daisy shape. Split the eight petals in half with a scalpel. Round each tip with the scalpel. Roll each petal with a cocktail stick. Pull a ball tool from the tip of each petal towards the centre. Turn the flower over and ball one or two petals so that they will curl in the opposite direction to give a more natural effect.

12 Moisten the base of the dried cone with some gum arabic and place the wire through the centre of the daisy. Gently stroke the flower into place allowing some petals to fall back and some to fall forwards over the centre of the cone for a natural effect. For the calyx, cut out a smaller daisy shape. Repeat the same process and attach to the back of the flower.

▼ *The nappy pin is made in two parts. The bow tie is finished with a ball for the knot.*

13 For the buds, ball the flowers so that the petals completely cover the cone. For the tiniest buds, just cut out a calyx and cover the small central cone. Dust the inner edge of the petals surrounding the centre a yellowish green; also the very centre of the flower and the edge of the calyx at the back of the flower.

14 To make marshmallow buds, take a pea-sized piece of paste. Pull a 28-gauge wire into the paste, and roll the top to form a cone. With the tweezers pinch three lines from the base of the cone to the top of the calyx. Roll out paste in the same colour green and cut out a shape using a snowdrop cutter. Use a ball tool to widen the petals. Place on a piece of foam and stroke the petals inwards. Ball the centre to pull the petals up tightly. Pinch each tip and place on the back of the cone.

◀ *Split each of the daisy's eight petals. Roll and ball the edges.*

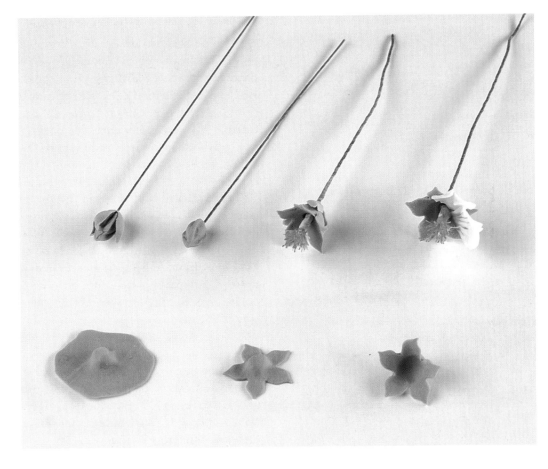

◀ *The marshmallow buds and flowers are made with a snowdrop cutter.*

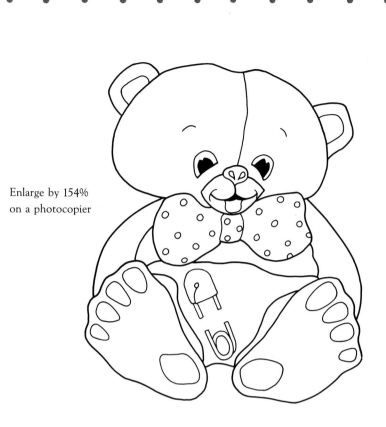

Enlarge by 154%
on a photocopier

▼ *If making the flowers seems too difficult,
substitute a fabric spray.*

15 For the larger bud, take a pea-sized piece of pale pink paste. Form a cone as before. With a scalpel, cut into the cone, pressing against the thumb while doing so, to form a thin edge. Repeat four times around the bud then twist the bud. Roll out some green flower paste and cut out a five-pointed calyx. Ball to thin the edges. Place the ball tool on each sepal tip and pull towards the centre. When attached, place on the final snowdrop shape.

16 To make the marshmallow flower, create stamens by wrapping fine cotton around two fingers at least 30 times. Attach a 26-gauge wire to each end of the loop and twist tightly. Cut the loop in half. Wrap some white stemwrap around the base of the stamens and wire. Dust with pale pink, moisten the tips of the stamens with gum arabic and insert into pale cream/yellow dust. Separate any stamens that become stuck together.

17 For the inner calyx, form a Mexican hat by taking a ball of paste and pinching all around the edges. Roll the edges with a cocktail stick until thin but leave a thick dimple in the middle. Use the calyx cutter to cut out the calyx shape. Ball and soften the edges. Gently insert a ball tool into the centre of the dimple and rotate to cup. Pull the stamens into this cup. Place the outer calyx (snowdrop) shape on as before. For the petals, using the pale pink paste, roll out really finely. Cut out five petals using a heart-shaped cutter. Ball each petal quite firmly to create movement. Attach to the space between each sepal. When dry, paint deep V-shaped colour at base of the petals with extra fine vein lines. Dust over this area with a slightly darker pink when the paint is dry to eradicate any harsh lines. When all the flowers are complete, wire them together into a crescent-shaped spray.

Benjamin

This sturdy blue cradle cake has a rustic look which is very appealing. For a girl, it could be made in pink or white.

CAKE AND DECORATION

19 x 30cm (7½ x 12 in) oblong Madeira or fruit cake · apricot glaze · 875g (1¾ lb) marzipan (almond paste) · 1.25kg (2½ lb) blue sugarpaste 500g (1 lb) white sugarpaste · small amount of royal icing · 500g (1 lb) flower paste or 250g (8 oz) Mexican paste · blueberry and grape violet food colourings · assorted paste colours · 1m (1 yd) narrow ribbon for hanging dummy · 1m (1 yd) ribbon for board edge

EQUIPMENT

30 x 35cm (12 x 14 in) oblong cakeboard · piping tubes (tips) · clay gun · ball tool · templates (see pages 68 and 78)

1 Cover the cakeboard with white sugarpaste and dry. Cover shaped cake with marzipan, then blue sugarpaste. While the paste is still soft, use a clean steel rule to indent and mark divisions representing strips of wood across the top of the cake and on both sides. For the rocker and posts, add 50 per cent flower paste or Mexican paste (modelling paste without the addition of the sugarpaste). The colour of the paste will now be much lighter than that on the cake; so add some blueberry and a touch of grape violet until the colours match.

2 Make the templates for the cradle from thin card. Slide the card under the cake so that a line can be drawn around the edges. The rocker should now fit snugly to the cake. Remove the card and cut out the shape of the rocker. Similarly, slide the left and right post shapes under each cake side and draw a line along the side of the cake.

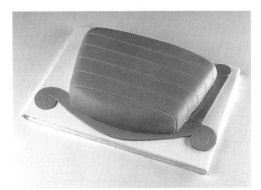

▲ *Slide the template under the cake to make the posts and rocker fit snugly.*

3 Roll out the paste 5mm (¼ in) deep. Cut around the base templates and butt against the cake as shown. Indent the curved line on each end of the rocker and knobs on top of each post. Cut out the upper rocker and remaining two posts and repeat the indentations. Leave to dry. Keep turning the sections so that they dry quickly and uniformly.

4 Make a thick sausage of paste to hold up the rocker at each end. This will support the shape. Keeping it flat, attach with royal icing. Pipe a generous amount of blue royal icing between the rocker and the cake, again to support and strengthen. Attach the two upper posts with royal icing. Pipe royal icing underneath the posts to strengthen them. Leave to dry.

5 Cut out the pink elephants. Cut out the ears from white paste and the top edge of the ear from pink. Cut out their blankets from a darker shade of pink. Do not attach to the cake at this stage but leave to dry on a non-

Enlarge by 154% on a photocopier

stick surface. When dry, paint on the ears. Mark in the eyes, the creases on the tummy and the trunk. When dry, attach the elephants to the cake.

6 Place a single-hole disc into a clay gun and push through some blue paste (the same colour as the cake). Attach the string of paste around the edge of the rocker. Stamp out the name using alphabet cutters and place on the rocker (see page 9 for alternative methods of lettering).

7 Mix some sugarpaste with the same amount of flower paste. Cut out the blanket shape in white. Ball and thin the edge. Attach to the top of the cradle. Drape it over one post. Lift and twist the edges to give a natural effect.

8 For the patchwork, take a walnut-sized piece of paste and roll into a sausage shape. Flatten in the hands so that the uppermost part of the shape is rounded. Make several more and butt the next shape to the previous one so

that it fits snugly. Work around the edge of the blanket leaving a 1cm (½ in) border. Mix pale colours of pink, blue and white. When the sugarpaste is dry, paint on the different patchwork patterns as shown.

9 For the dummy, make a sausage shape from flesh-coloured paste. Thin one end by rolling the sausage between the two index fingers. Cut out a disc of paste 4cm (1½ in) wide by 1.5mm (¹⁄₁₆ in) thick. Indent a hole in the middle of the disc with a ball tool. Roll out a long, thin roll of paste. Cut each end at an angle and butt together to form a circle.

10 When dry, attach to the back of the disc using royal icing, then attach the dummy, also with royal icing. When the royal icing has dried, thread a ribbon through the loop of the dummy. Hang around the top of the post and attach with a few spots of royal icing to keep it in place.

▼ *Apply rounded pieces of paste to the blanket. Paint patchwork designs when dry.*

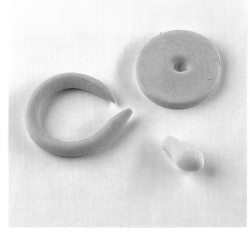

▲ *The dummy is composed of three pieces. When assembled, thread onto ribbon.*

Sleeping Beauty

The curly head of a sweetly sleeping baby is just visible under the frills and folds of a beautiful quilt.

CAKE AND DECORATION

20 x 15cm (8 x 6 in) oblong cake · apricot glaze
1.25kg (2½ lb) marzipan (almond paste) · 2kg (4 lb) sugarpaste · mint green and spruce green paste colours · small amount of royal icing · gum tragacanth · assorted food colourings · gum arabic cornflour (cornstarch) · 30g (1 oz) modelling paste (bas relief paste) · Garrett frill paste (see page 8) 1m (1 yd) of 3mm (⅛ in) ribbon · 1m (1 yd) ribbon for board edge

EQUIPMENT

28 x 23cm (11 x 9 in) oblong cakeboard · silicone parchment · Garrett frill cutter · large ball tool doll's head mould · anger tool · fine paintbrushes piping tubes (tips) · templates (see page 75)

1 Cover the cake with marzipan. Mix a small amount of mint green and a small amount of spruce green into the sugarpaste to form a subtle *eau de nil* colour for the sugarpaste. Cover the cake. Pipe a snail trail around the base of the cake. Add a band of 3mm (⅛ in) ribbon.

2 To prepare the paste for the drape add 1 tsp of gum tragacanth to the sugarpaste. Leave overnight to make

the paste easier to handle. Make a template by measuring how far down the side the drape is required, across the top of the cake and then the equal depth the opposite side. Repeat for the length of the cake. Cut out the template using the silicone parchment.

3 Roll out the paste very finely. Keep moving it so that it does not stick to the work surface. The paste should be thin enough so that a patterned piece of paper placed underneath can be easily defined. Cut out the desired size. Pick it up carefully using the flat of the hand and place over the arm. Drape over the cake – no glue or water is necessary to attach it. Take time to arrange some natural-looking folds in the paste so that it resembles a bed sheet. Allow to dry.

4 Make a template for the green blanket which sits inside the top curve of the cake. Roll out the paste and cut and place onto the cake. Trim the edges with a scalpel so that they are straight. Allow to dry.

5 Apply another blanket in white 5mm (¼ in) inside the green blanket. Allow to dry. Using the template for the folded piece of blanket,

▲ *The straight edge of the green blanket contrasts with the other frills and curves.*

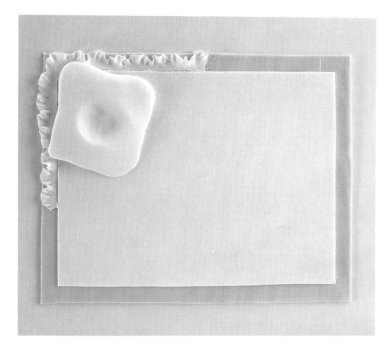

6 For the pillow, take a small piece of sugarpaste. Roll into a ball, flatten and tweak out the top two corners for the pillow. Place on the bed at an angle. Using a large ball tool, indent a shape for the head. Place another thin frill around three edges of the pillow.

7 For the baby's head an easy-to-make mould can be used. Most cake specialist shops sell small angels or dolls, or a mould can be taken from a child's toy if preferred. Simply push the doll's head into some modelling, gelatine or flower paste. Colour some modelling paste with paprika and a tiny spot of melon to make flesh colour. Form a ball, making sure there are no creases or tucks visible on the face. Dust lightly with cornflour so that the paste will not stick.

8 Place the paste into the mould. The face should now be clearly indented. Improve on certain features such as the nose; place the narrow end

▲ *Tweak out the corners of the pillow and place at an angle. Indent as shown.*

lay it on the corner of the bed and scribe a line across the corner. On the green edge in that top corner, place a thin Garrett frill. Allow the frill to continue 5mm (¼ in) past the scribed line.

▶ *Form the baby's rough body shape, with feet and an arm, but take care with the hand.*

of the anger tool into each nostril and open slightly, lifting the tool during the process, so that the nose becomes more upturned and cute. Deepen the area between the corner of the eye and nose, to make the nose slimmer. Cut between the lips with a scalpel and open the mouth with an anger tool to make it more shapely.

9 For the ear, see *Baby with Orchids,* page 20. Look at someone's ear while forming the shape. Form the outer edge by pressing an anger tool into a flattened ball of paste and pushing it against the thumb. Repeat this technique for the shapes within the ear. Attach to the side of the baby's head with gum arabic. Insert the thin end of the anger tool through the ear and into the head to form the hole in the ear. Glue the head in place into the indented area on the pillow. Pipe in some hair using some royal icing.

10 Using sugarpaste, form a rough body shape with a narrow upper area and a larger, deeper lower half. Form one left foot and one right foot and butt against the bottom. Make an arm by rolling a piece of sugarpaste, bending it and opening up the sleeve area so that the hand can be inserted. All these shapes will be covered by the quilt so it is only necessary to create an impression of the body.

11 More care needs to be taken with the hand. Take a small piece of paste and form a spade shape. With a pair of scissors, cut out a small V for the thumb. Make four further cuts in the shape that is left. Pull each finger using the same technique as for pulled flowers. Round off each fingertip. Place a ball tool on the hand at the tip of the fingers and stroke towards the palm to curve the fingers. Twist the hand at an angle so that it takes on a natural, sideways position. Place the hand inside the sleeve and put the arm on the upper body with the hand on the pillow near the face.

12 Roll out the top quilt quite finely using white sugarpaste. Carefully arrange over the baby so that the body shape is clearly visible. Use a finger to smooth the paste over the feet so that they don't become lost. Trim any excess paste around the edges.

13 For the turned-back area, use the templates to cut out a triangular white and a triangular green piece of paste. Place the green paste onto the white paste, allowing a border of 5mm (¼ in). Gently roll the top edge of the white paste over the green and place over the top cover of the quilt and body of the baby. Again, be careful to smooth the edges around the body.

14 Paint the pattern on the quilt using an assortment of paste colours. Continue the narrow frill around the edge of the quilt. Pipe a small tricot pattern around the edge of the draped sheet using royal icing.

▼ *Only the top of the head and the fingers are visible on the finished cake.*

Templates

FRILLED CRADLE
Page 37

INNER CRADLE SHAPE

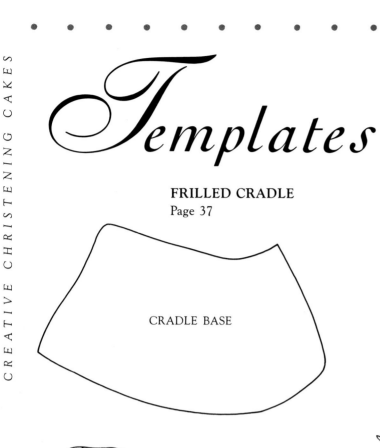

CRADLE BASE

LOWER DRAPE

BLANKET

TOP SHEET (NEAR FACE)
Allow extra paste to turn
edge under all round

CRADLE GARLAND
Page 13

Enlarge all templates by 154% on a photocopier

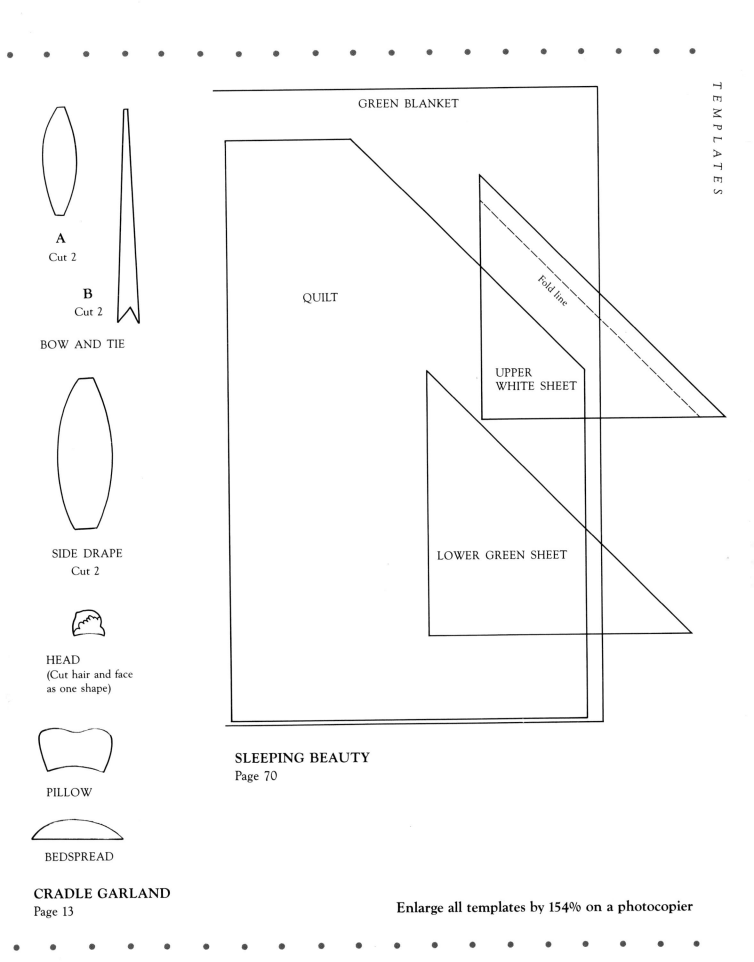

A
Cut 2

B
Cut 2

BOW AND TIE

SIDE DRAPE
Cut 2

HEAD
(Cut hair and face
as one shape)

PILLOW

BEDSPREAD

CRADLE GARLAND
Page 13

GREEN BLANKET

QUILT

Fold line

UPPER
WHITE SHEET

LOWER GREEN SHEET

SLEEPING BEAUTY
Page 70

Enlarge all templates by 154% on a photocopier

CUTWORK TEDDY
Page 40

INDENT

INDENT

A COSY CHICK
Page 49

DRESS

COLLAR

LEFT SLEEVE

RIGHT SLEEVE

BABY IN LACE
Page 42

Enlarge all templates by 154% on a photocopier

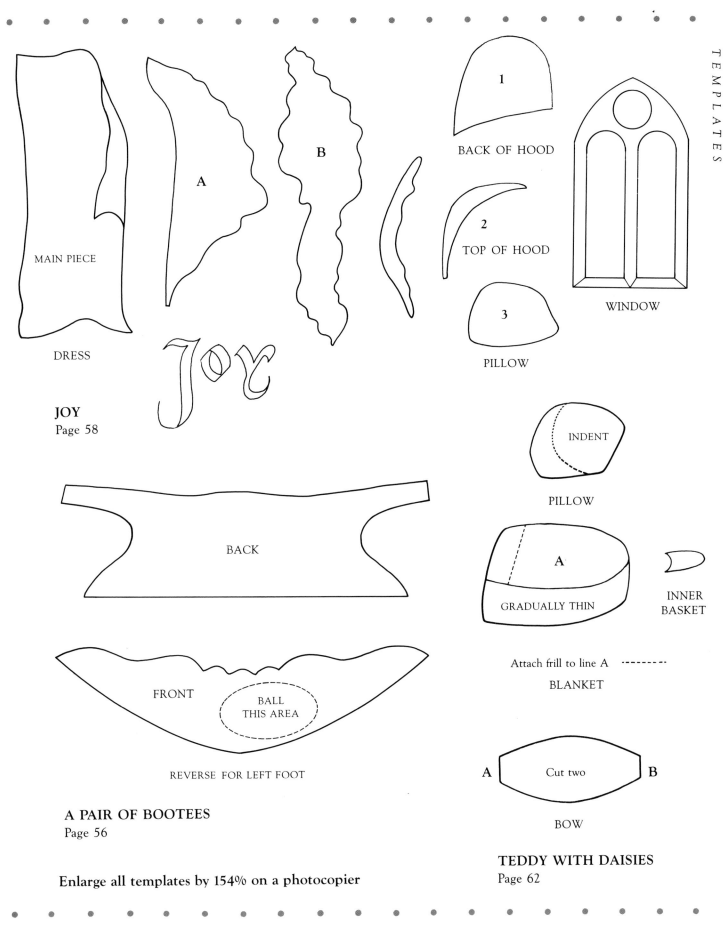

BACK OF HOOD

1

TOP OF HOOD

2

WINDOW

PILLOW

3

MAIN PIECE

DRESS

A

B

JOY
Page 58

INDENT

PILLOW

A

GRADUALLY THIN

INNER BASKET

BACK

Attach frill to line A ---------
BLANKET

FRONT

BALL THIS AREA

REVERSE FOR LEFT FOOT

A   Cut two   B

BOW

A PAIR OF BOOTEES
Page 56

TEDDY WITH DAISIES
Page 62

Enlarge all templates by 154% on a photocopier

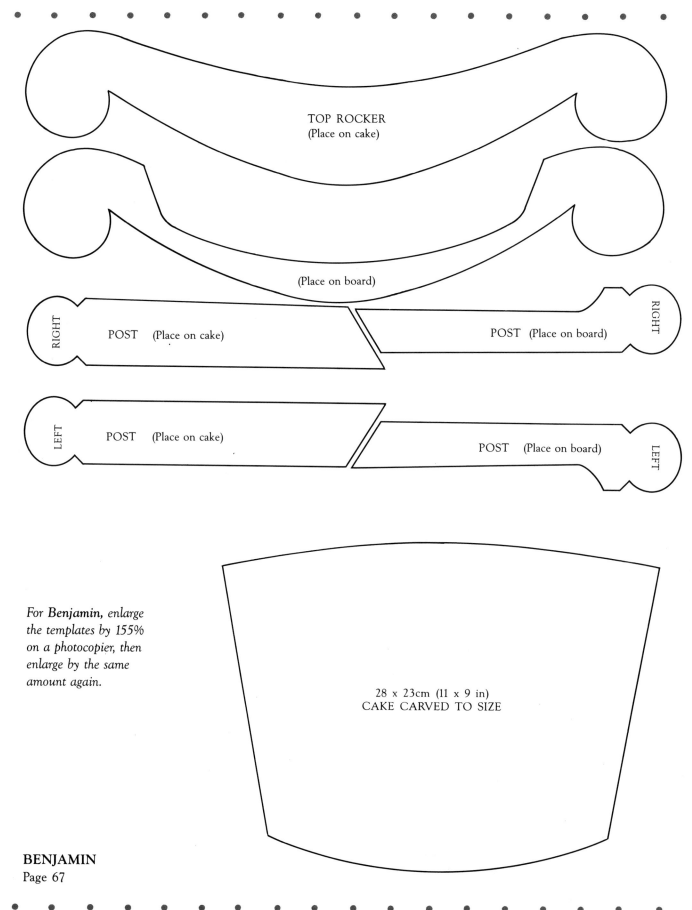

TOP ROCKER
(Place on cake)

(Place on board)

RIGHT
POST (Place on cake)

POST (Place on board)
RIGHT

LEFT
POST (Place on cake)

POST (Place on board)
LEFT

*For Benjamin, enlarge
the templates by 155%
on a photocopier, then
enlarge by the same
amount again.*

28 x 23cm (11 x 9 in)
CAKE CARVED TO SIZE

BENJAMIN
Page 67

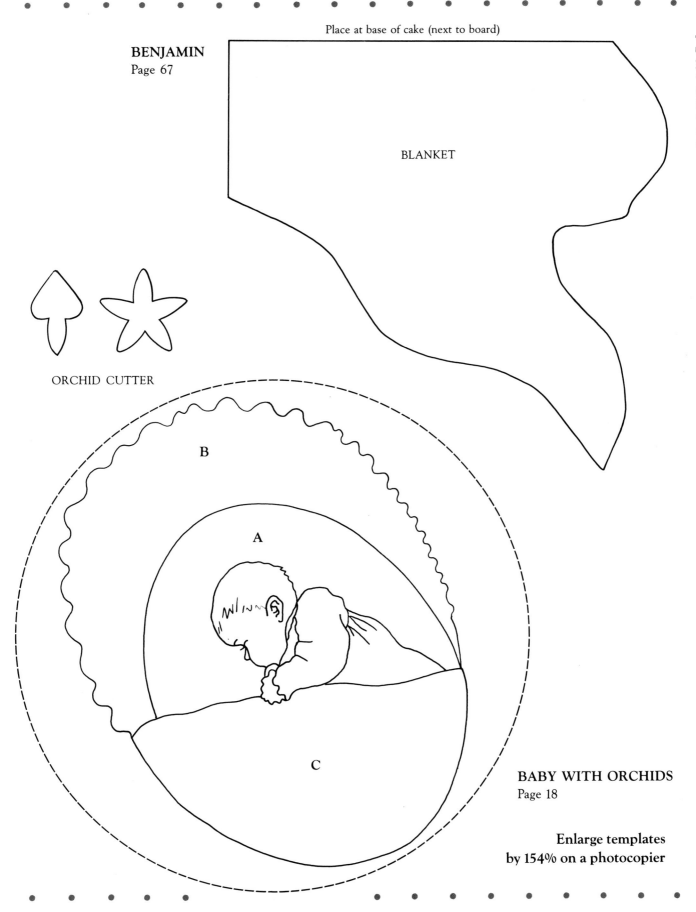

Place at base of cake (next to board)

BENJAMIN
Page 67

BLANKET

ORCHID CUTTER

B

A

C

BABY WITH ORCHIDS
Page 18

**Enlarge templates
by 154% on a photocopier**

Index

Acknowledgements

The publishers would like to thank the following suppliers:

Cake Art Ltd
Venture Way,
Crown Estate,
Priorswood,
Taunton, TA2 8DE

Guy, Paul and Co. Ltd
Unit B4,
Foundry Way,
Little End Road,
Eaton Socon,
Cambs, PE19 3JH

Squires Kitchen
Squires House,
3 Waverley Lane,
Farnham,
Surrey, GU9 8BB

**Anniversary House
(Cake Decorations) Ltd**
Unit 16,
Elliott Road,
West Howe Industrial Estate,
Bournemouth, BH11 8LZ

The author would like to thank:
J. F. Renshaw Ltd.,
Crown Street,
Liverpool, L8 7RF
for supplying Regalice